official guide to

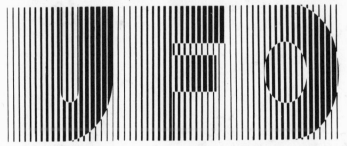

SIGHTINGS

official guide to

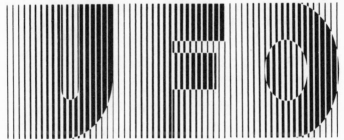

SIGHTINGS

Carl Sifakis

A DRAKE PUBLICATION
STERLING PUBLISHING CO., INC.   NEW YORK

Published by Sterling Publishing Co., Inc.
Two Park Avenue
New York, N.Y. 10016.

Library of Congress Cataloging in Publication Data

Sifakis, Carl.
    Official guide to UFO sightings.

    1. Flying saucers. I. Title.
TL789.S523   001.9'42'0973   78-7091
ISBN 0-8069-8850-9

Printed in the United States of America

To Stefan

CONTENTS

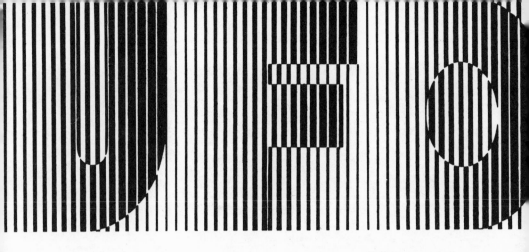

Chapter 1
WE BELIEVE!

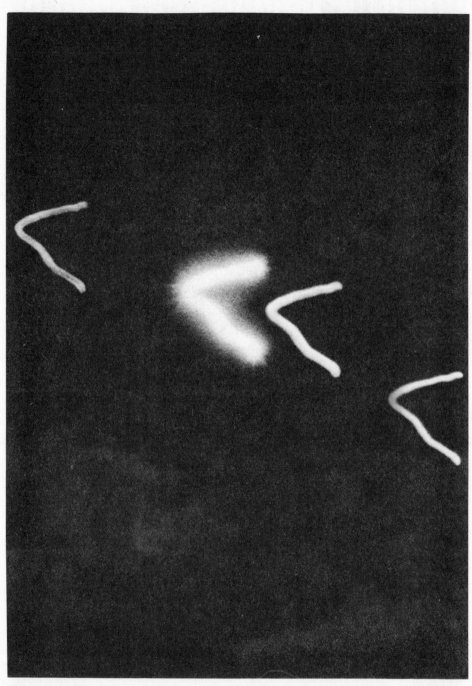

This photo of four strange lights was taken in Columbus, Ohio, during that state's great flap in 1973 when at least 150 persons, including Governor John J. Gilligan, saw UFOs in various parts of the state.

Chapter 1

WE BELIEVE!

Do UFOs — unidentified flying objects, flying saucers, what-have-you — really exist?

Ask the American people. As far back as 1971, a poll by *Industrial Research* revealed that of 2700 engineers and professional scientists questioned, 54 percent declared that UFOs "definitely or probably" exist.

Ask the average layman. In a Gallup poll released in November, 1973, 51 percent of the people polled were found to believe that UFOs are real. Fifty-one percent . . . over 100 million people. That's an awful lot of "crazies." And an even more startling figure is this: 11 percent said that they had themselves seen a UFO. That's well over 20 million people, an awful lot of "real crazies."

For years, Ufologists have claimed that military and government agencies have been engaged in actively suppressing or distorting evidence in thousands of UFO reports. Yet, despite these debunking efforts, belief in UFOs continues to grow. Lending credence to this wave of believers is that more and more prominent persons are willing to step forward and publicly take a stand.

"I don't laugh at people anymore when they say they've seen UFOs, because I've seen one myself." That was Jimmy Carter speaking at a Washington press conference on May 11, 1975. It was a remarkable statement for a presidential candidate to make. Carter risked being labeled a "nut." Yet he said it because he felt the time had come for straight talk on UFOs.

Carter's UFO experience occurred on September 13, 1973, while he was standing outside a Leary, Georgia, meeting hall just before he was to address the Lion's Club. Later, Carter told reporters in Dublin, Georgia, that "it was a very remarkable sight. It was about 30 degrees above the horizon and looked about as large as the moon. It got smaller and changed to a reddish color and then got larger again. It was a very sober occasion. It was obviously there and obviously unidentified."

Then there is the comment of John J. Gilligan, made during his term as governor of Ohio. He told Statehouse newsmen on October 17, 1973, that he and his wife, Katie, "saw one the other night, so help me." The gover-

nor went on to say that on the previous Monday night they had been driving home from a weekend at their summer home at Lake LeeLanau, Michigan, on Route 23 near Ann Arbor when they saw the UFO.

"It was a vertical beam of light, amber-colored, and we watched it for
about thirty-five minutes. It couldn't have been a reflection. It would
fade out and get bright. I frankly don't know what it was. I'm absolutely
serious. I saw this. It was not a plane, it was not a bird, it didn't wear a
cape, and I really don't know what it was."

Heavyweight champion Muhammed Ali claimed that he had seen a
UFO while training in New York's Central Park in 1972. According to the
champ: "I was out jogging just before sunrise. It was the day before one
of my fights and I happened to glance up and see this bright light coming
up from Manhattan's towering skyline. It seemed to be just hovering
there, watching me. The thing grew in intensity, moving closer until it
just stood out like a huge electric lightbulb circling overhead in the sky."

Can Ali be believed, considering his notorious habit of putting on the
press? There were other witnesses to the event, including Ali's trainer and
a newspaperman who was covering Ali's fight preparations.

Arthur Godfrey is another well-known personality who has gone on record as having encountered a UFO. On his regular nationwide program,
Godfrey told of his startling experience. It had occurred at night while he
was flying near Philadelphia in his private executive plane with co-pilot
Frank Munciello. Suddenly a brightly lighted object came into view off
their right wing, and Godfrey had to bank to avoid a collision. Then the
UFO veered and took a position on the left wing of Godfrey's plane. Godfrey tried to pull away but the UFO stayed with every maneuver.

"It stayed there on the left wing, no matter what I did," Godfrey
said. Finally, after several frightening minutes, the strange craft veered
off and vanished. Godfrey freely admitted that both he and co-pilot
Munciello had been thoroughly shaken by the experience.

At the time of the Godfrey incident, the U.S. Air Force was well along
in its campaign to repudiate and deride UFO sightings. However, no real
effort was made to discredit Godfrey. He was a national figure and considered a top-rate pilot, having flown Navy, Air Force, and commercial
planes, including jets. And he was, after all, a colonel in the Air Force
Reserve.

Nor has Godfrey been the only trained observer to spot a UFO. In addition to reports by a number of skilled pilots, there have been numerous
sightings by astronauts. On Gemini 4, astronaut James McDivitt observed
a cylindrical object with a protuberance. He also observed a bright light

Muhammed Ali told of his UFO sighting: "It seemed to be just hovering there, watching me."

moving at a level higher than that of the Gemini spacecraft. On Gemini 7, astronaut Frank Borman saw what he referred to as a "bogey" flying in formation with the spacecraft.

Apollo XII astronauts Pete Conrad, Dick Gordon, and Alan Bean declared that a UFO accompanied them to within 132,000 miles of the moon, or about halfway to it. Were some amused outer space observers watching to see if these puny earthling space missions would succeed?

The astronaut probably most outspoken about his belief in flying saucers is Ed Mitchell. He declared at a recent conference concerning flying saucers: "Gentlemen, we all know that UFOs are real. The question is, where do they come from?"

We may not know the answer to that yet, but we know where they have been seen: in every state in the Union.

Astronaut Edgar Mitchell has said, "We all know UFOs are real. The question is, where do they come from?"

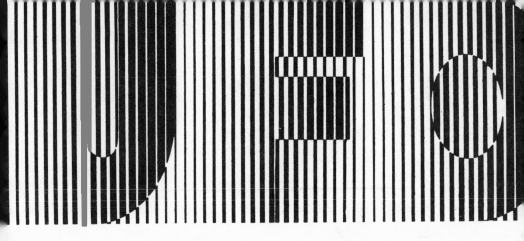

Chapter 2

UFO Q's AND A's

Chapter 2
UFO Q's AND A's

Close encounters of all three kinds have occurred all over this country. This book will tell the UFO buff planning his vacation, or any other kind of trip, where to look for the markings of sights of extraterrestrial visitors and their crafts, and what evidence is still available that he may see for himself. He may even be able to contact and talk to some of the witnesses who have seen such "visitations" with their own eyes. Because there have been sightings in every state, it is possible to map out a "trail" of UFO markers that will conicide handily with one's travel plans and bring the wonders of the universe within the perimeters of a family experience.

However, before going on to a geographical listing, it may be well to consider the broad view of UFOs by answering the most commonly asked questions about them.

When did UFOs first appear and who saw them?

Reports of UFOs go back through the ages, to biblical times and earlier. In this country, mountain men living among the Indians around 1800 heard stories of giant, man-like "crazy bears" put down on Indian hunting grounds by "small moons." In the 1890s, a large number of Americans witnessed the flight of "airships" all over America. The mayors of San Francisco and Oakland, California, reported seeing glowing, cigar-shaped aircraft. In Texarkana, Arkansas, Judge Lawrence A. Byrne said he happened upon the airship and its occupants. He is quoted in the *Daily Texarkanian* of April 25, 1897: "It was manned by three men who spoke a foreign language, but judging from their looks, I would take them to be Japanese."

In the 1930s, "ghost fliers" were the rage in many parts of the world. The New York *Times* of December 27, 1933, devoted a column to the "mystery airplane" that was heard over the city during a raging snowstorm. The airplanes of that period were not capable of flying in blizzards.

Modern day UFOs are considered to have had their origin on June 24, 1947, when private pilot Kenneth Arnold spotted nine disc-like crafts over Mt. Rainier. He estimated their speed at about 1700 mph. Newsmen tabbed the UFOs "flying saucers" and the rage was on. Hollywood began grinding out movies, magazines began publishing photographs of them, and some very curious and serious people began investigating them.

Was there ever an official explanation of these disc-shaped objects?

The Arnold sighting in 1947 is still in the "unexplained" category, but it and many others that followed eventually prompted the Air Force's Air Technical Intelligence Center (ATIC) to start Project Blue Book, a top-priority, high-security investigation of subsequent flying saucer reports.

Is Project Blue Book still investigating UFOs?

No. The Air Force terminated its UFO investigations in December, 1969. There are those who insist a top secret investigation still goes on.

Did Project Blue Book "solve" all the cases it investigated?

Several Ufologists insist that many of the Air Force's solutions were spurious. In addition, of the 15,000 reports in Project Blue Book files, some 3000 were classified as "unsolved." Put another way, there were at least 3000 inconclusive conclusions.

Didn't the Air Force conduct another major study of UFOs?

Yes. The Air Force commissioned a two-year scientific study of UFOs, conducted under the directorship of Dr. Edward U. Condon, a prominent American physicist. It was begun in 1966 and its findings were released to the public in January, 1969.

According to the Condon Report, there was no evidence to justify a belief that extraterrestrial visitors have penetrated our skies, and not enough evidence to warrant any further scientific investigation.

Were the findings unanimous?

Hardly. A former member of the project later co-authored a book charging that the entire study might have been organized — without the knowledge of most of its staff — for the distinct purpose of diverting attention from the real nature of UFOs. The most damaging, and surely the most embarrassing, charge against the Condon Report was the disclosure of the notorious "Low Memo." Dr. Condon had many other duties and never devoted his full time to the study. As his project administra-

An Air Force photo of a "physically fabricated" UFO.

tor he appointed Robert Low, who really ran the show. (The study is better labeled the "Low Report.")

Whether Low was ever capable of conducting an unbiased investigation is open to question. In a memo written on August 9, 1966, some three months before the project even formally began, Low said, "The trick would be, I think, to describe the project so that, to the public, it would appear a totally objective study but, to the scientific community, would present the image of a group of nonbelievers trying their best to be objective but having an almost zero expectation of finding a saucer."

Is there really any reason to doubt the Air Force's claim that it terminated its UFO investigations in 1969?

Let's just say that many informed people are skeptical. Right now, they insist, there is an ongoing investigation that is classified most secret. And they say that certain key high-ranking personnel within the Air Force know a lot more about UFOs than they are willing to tell the general public.

Doesn't that statement smack of paranoia? If there was any truth to it, wouldn't someone have spoken out by now?

Quite a few already have. Major Donald E. Keyhoe (USMC, Ret.), in his book, *Aliens from Space — The Real Story of Unidentified Flying Objects*, lists some: "Col. Howard Strand, Detachment Commander, Air National Guard Base, Battle Creek, Michigan: During flights in F94 all-weather interceptors Colonel Strand had three encounters with UFOs. 'They were no figments of imagination. Too many intelligent, competent observers have reported UFOs. My conclusion is that this is a reconnaissance by an advanced civilization. I urge a congressional investigation of UFOs and the military secrecy surrounding them.'

"Col. Joseph Bryan, USAF, Ret., Special Assistant to the Secretary of the Air Force during early UFO operations and later assigned to the staff of Gen. Lauris Norstad: After stating that he was aware of many cases of UFO sightings and radar trackings by competent observers, Colonel Bryan added: 'The UFOs are interplanetary devices systematically observing the Earth, either manned or remote-controlled or both. Information on UFOs has been officially withheld. This policy is wrong and dangerous.'

"Lt. Col. James McAshan, USAFR: 'In concealing the evidence of UFO operations the Air Force is making a serious mistake. The public should be informed as to the facts.'

"Maj. Dewey Fournet, Former AF HQ monitor of the UFO Project: 'The AF withholds UFO information, including sighting reports.'

"Former AF Maj. F. Thomas Lowrey, a graduate of Carnegie Institute of Technology, with World War II service as an engineer at the Aircraft Laboratory, Wright-Patterson AFB: 'I am thoroughly convinced that the "flying saucers" come from some extraterrestrial source. I cannot understand the AF policy of pretending they do not exist.' "

But if UFOs really do exist and are in fact intelligently guided craft of some kind, why haven't any of them crashed? Surely, no matter how advanced the technology, wouldn't there have been malfunctions during all the years they have been zipping around our skies?

No quarrel with that. Nobody's perfect, not even the humans, creatures, or "things" that pilot or guide UFOs. There are indeed recorded incidents of UFOs that have crashed.

Then why don't we have any physical evidence of the existence of UFOs? If we know that some of them have crashed, shouldn't we have a piece of one of them?

Again, no quarrel. The only problem is the "we." Parts of UFOs are in someone's possession, but they are not available for public scrutiny.

Well, where are the pieces and why haven't they been shown to the public?

We don't know where the pieces or chunks are but we do know who is guarding them. We haven't been allowed to see them because the UFO cover-up is a multi-government affair, evidently. Let's consider just one case. In 1952 a UFO was reported to have crashed somewhere among the Spitzbergen Islands, about halfway between the North Pole and Norway. A combined group of experts from Norway, the United States, and Britain hurried to investigate the strange craft.

On September 4, 1955, newsmen conducted an interview with the head of the board of inquiry, which later appeared in various European newspapers. According to Colonel Gernod Darnbyl, head of the board of inquiry that was conducted by the Norwegian General Staff: "It [the UFO] has — this we wish to state emphatically — not been built by any country on Earth. The materials used in the construction are completely unknown to all experts who participated in the investigation."

At the time, it was understood that the Norwegians intended to publish an in-depth report following the completed investigation. Col. Darnbyl did add, however, that the report would be held up until "some of the sensational facts have been discussed with the United States and British experts." Needless to say, no report was ever issued. The inescapable conclusion is that the United States and Britain clamped a lid of secrecy on the entire matter.

What about other UFO chunks?

In his book, *Flying Saucers — Serious Business*, the late Frank Edwards, a highly respected news commentator, stated that several fragments from UFOs had been found in many parts of the world. For example, the Canadian government was said to be holding a 3000-pound chunk of UFO metal in a secret, heavily-guarded storehouse. Scores of Americans have been reported to have found flying saucer hardware. These objects have tended to be swallowed up by a veil of military censorship (there has been speculation that finders have been silenced by being told they have found part of a United States secret weapon) or the finder is called a hoaxer and his chunk a phony. Because of this, such discoveries receive only "squib" coverage in many newspapers.

If I discover a strange piece of metal that I believe may have come from a UFO, what can I do?

You can, of course, notify the government. Naturally, when an Air Force Intelligence Officer turns up and requests the object, it will be rather hard to refuse. And if you hand it over, you can forget about it. Another option is to turn it over to a reliable civilian UFO investigatory group. (See the listing in the Appendix.) Instead of being branded a faker or a nut — unless you are one — you will get an honest analysis.

If UFOs are real, why is there such a wide disparity in their reported descriptions?

There are many similarities in many cases, even from one continent to another, but there are also many differences. Why does a 1979 Pontiac look different than a 1974 Pontiac? Just as automobiles change from year to year, it is possible that UFOs undergo design alterations. Another explanation that cannot be overlooked is the belief held by many leading Ufologists that UFOs visiting this planet come from more than one source in space.

This photograph was taken by a newsman in Sicuani, in southern Peru, near Puno.

A Polaroid photo of a UFO sighted thirty-four miles east of Lima, Peru, in a secluded valley near the Rimac River.

Are UFOs hostile?

Although most Ufologists say no, there are occasional reports of injuries and even deaths attributed to UFOs. One man who claimed he was a UFO "contactee" died of mysterious radiation poisoning a few months after his reported encounter. Most Ufologists attribute isolated acts of apparent violence to accidents. If UFOs have been around as long as some observers think and haven't been violent in all that time, it hardly makes sense that they'll turn mean at this stage. Of course, "hostility" can be in the eyes of the observed. If you believe that being watched is a hostile act, then UFOs are definitely hostile.

Have we been hostile to UFOs?

Definitely. There are numerous reports of UFOs being fired on and hit by both the military and civilians.

What about contact — strange encounters of the third kind?

Several persons have made such a claim. Many are obviously lying. The most prominent of the early contactees was George Adamski, who claimed he was bringing messages of brotherhood and peace from space beings. Most of the top Ufologists consider Adamski a hoaxer and a cultist. Many, like Adamski, have written books about their alleged experiences, but few are believed. As Frank Edwards wrote: "The only flights human beings have ever made in UFOs appear to be flights of fancy." Since then, numerous contactee cases have cropped up that are not so easily dismissed.

As to the sightings by astronauts: Could they really have seen other man-made satellites?

According to NASA, none of these sightings involved other man-made satellites. NASA has never released any explanation of what these objects were.

So many astronomers scan the skies; do they spot UFOs?

Some astronomers have: Dr. Seymour Hess; Frank Halstead, head of Darling Observatory for over twenty-five years; Dr. H. Percy Wilkins; and Bart Bok of Australia's Mt. Stomio Observatory.

But that's only a handful. If UFOs are real, shouldn't all astronomers with telescopes have seen them?

Not at all. Telescopes are built for viewing objects at very great distances. Anything flying at close range is simply impossible to see with a telescope, including a commercial airliner.

What countries have seen the most UFOs?

UFOs have apparently been seen by people in every nation in the world, most often over the more industrially developed countries. It could be that UFOs find more to see there, or it could be simply that communications are better in such countries and thus more reports are possible.

How are UFOs propelled?

The most common belief is that UFOs use antigravity devices. According to Dr. Hermann Oberth, a West German scientist who directed a UFO investigative commission, the mysterious craft are "conceived and directed by intelligent beings of a very high order, and they are propelled by distorting the gravitational field, converting gravity into usable energy."

Why aren't UFOs picked up on radar?

Unidentified "blips" have been tracked on radar thousands of times. One of the most famous trackings occurred in July, 1952, when a "squad" of UFOs buzzed the nation's capital. The sightings bumped the Democratic National Convention right out of the headlines.

What did we find out about this "squad" of UFOs?

Absolutely nothing except that they could outmaneuver our fastest jets, which went up after them.

Why are so many UFOs sighted near swamps and deserts?

Assuming UFOs are extraterrestrial in origin, it is easy to understand why they would search out such unpopulated areas. The operators would quite logically be under orders to carry out any emergency landings for inspections and repairs in the most isolated places possible.

Where else do UFO visitors like to go?

They seem to have a great appetite for areas near high-tension power

An unidentified flying object passes over the Hotel Washington in Lugano, Switzerland.

A controversial Brazilian UFO photo. Note that the lighting of the disc is clearly from the left, while the hillside indicates lighting from the right.

lines and large electrical power facilities. It may be that their purpose is to tap our power supply as a means of "refueling." This is not necessarily in conflict with the theory that UFOs are most likely propelled by anti-gravity methods. Such antigravity systems may involve electrical power in some way.

Could UFO refueling needs have something to do with our power black-outs?

Ufologists say yes. There seems to be strong evidence that many power blackouts, particularly the massive blackout of the Northeast in 1965, were accompanied by a flurry of UFO activity. In the big 1965 blackout, a UFO was reported in the very location where power company officials later pinpointed the source of the electrical failure.

Aren't most reports of UFO sightings made by "UFO nuts," or at least buffs — people who live and breathe flying saucers and "true believers" who attend UFO conventions and such?

Not at all. Only a very small number of the reports come from UFO fanatics. Most people who have reported sightings and encounters said they had never believed in flying saucers until they themselves had seen a UFO.

But let's face it: aren't most UFO sighters, if not fanatics, certainly of below-average intelligence?

Quite the opposite. Says Dr. J. Allen Hynek, former consultant of Project Blue Book and for years a skeptic himself: "The level of intelligence of the observers and reporters of UFOs is certainly at least average and, in many cases, decidedly above average. In some cases, embarrassingly above average."

If there is a UFO cover-up, wouldn't it have to involve other governments besides the United States?

Yes. The British government, for one.

Does that involve more than the Spitzbergen Islands incident?

Yes. There seems evidence that the British have investigated more than one piece of UFO wreckage. A clue to this was revealed by Dorothy Kilgallen, the late newspaper columnist and television personality. Shortly before her death, she wrote about a recent trip to England: "I can report today on a story that is positively spooky, not to mention chilling. British scientists and airmen, after examination of the wreckage of one mysterious flying ship, are convinced that these strange aerial objects are not optical illusions or Soviet inventions, but are actually flying saucers which originate on another planet. The source of my information is a British official of Cabinet rank, who prefers to remain unidentified.

"He says: 'We believe, on the basis of our inquiries thus far, that the saucers were staffed by small men — probably under four feet tall. It's frightening but there is no denying the flying saucers came from another planet.'

"This official quoted scientists as saying a flying ship of this type could not possibly have been constructed on Earth. The British government, I learned, is withholding an official report on the flying saucer examination at this time, possibly because it does not want to frighten the public. . . . "

If UFOs are from outer space, why not let the world know about it? Aren't people sophisticated enough to handle the news without panic?

That is a moot point. The feeling seems to be that a great many people on this planet would not be able to cope. The Orson Welles radio dramatization of *War of the Worlds* in 1938 and the reaction it caused would be child's play compared with what this news would produce in reality. There seems to be a fear that it would set off a rash of suicides around the world. Perhaps some experts are also afraid that economic chaos would ensue. The stability of the world's economy is based on one factor more than any other: No surprises. Business hates surprises and this would be a big one. Some experts also warn that any outer space beings would obviously be far more advanced than us, and they point out that whenever two uneven cultures mix, the weaker one perishes, as was the case of the white man and the American Indian.

Not all experts agree with this outlook, insisting that "human" faults are not necessarily part of a space being's makeup. Dr. Robert Jastrow, director of NASA's Goddard Institute for Space Studies in New York City, considers it "really nonsensical" that alien beings would have warlike intentions. He feels that space beings would welcome the fresh ideas of earthlings, since our planet is much younger than the rest of the galaxy. He predicts that the alien creatures will be so advanced that "their command of natural forces and communication would be far beyond our comprehension." With these tools, according to Dr. Jastrow, "they would give

Gen. Douglas A. MacArthur told the 1962 West Point graduating class that the nations of Earth would some day have to unite against attacks by inhabitants of other planets. "We speak of ultimate conflict between the united human race and the sinister forces of some other planetary galaxy."

us subtle guidance on our morality and behavior so as to prepare us for crossing the threshold and entering the galactic community."

What about all the photographs of UFOs? Have any of them proved not to be fakes?

It is the curse of the UFO field that so many nuts and hoaxers are attracted to it. Many, many photographs have proved to be outright fakes and others pure honest mistakes, clearly attributable to natural, explainable phenomena. However, after the most careful expert scrutiny, many other pictures have been found to be completely unexplainable — except as UFOs.

Does the government plan to open any new UFO investigations to clear up the enigma once and for all?

Who says they ever stopped? John Marks, ex-government spook and co-author of *The CIA and the Cult of Intelligence*, once told a reporter that the super-secret agency has a very special office which examines UFO reports. According to another source, this office is in CIA Headquarters at Langley, Virginia, and is accessible only to persons who enter after obtaining special badges and being escorted past an obstruction known as "the blind man's barrier." Everyone who comes and goes is photographed; not even a top-secret clearance, by itself, will gain entrance.

In addition to all of this, the Defense Department is still recording reports of UFOs today. Thomas B. Ross, Assistant Secretary of Defense for Public Affairs, says the Defense Department has never stopped reporting UFOs that affect military installations. "I don't know how many such reports have been made or with what frequency," Ross says, "but clearly there are reports." Of course, Ross insists there is "no central office" that collects or studies UFO reports. "They are to be reported to the national military command center, to the Joint Chiefs of Staff, to the various pertinent commands, and they're treated there as any message would be treated." Add to the Ross statement this one from an Air Force spokesman: "No evidence has been presented to indicate that further investigation of UFOs by the Air Force is warranted. There is no likelihood of renewed Air Force involvement in this area." All this adds up, depending on one's viewpoint, to a stone wall or to the military "stonewalling" it.

Will the UFO riddle ever be solved?

Right now, that's up to the UFOs.

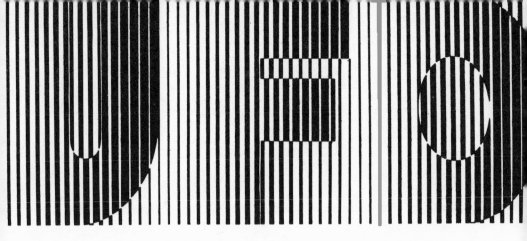

Chapter 3

"FLAP" AREAS

Chapter 3
"FLAP" AREAS

It happened in North Bergen, New Jersey, in January, 1975. Not really it
. . . *they*. There were many separate incidents.

Incident 1: At about 3:00 A.M. on a night mild for January, George
O'Barski was driving through North Hudson Park, listening to his car radio.
Suddenly the radio developed static and started to fade. Then O'Barski,
a liquor store manager although himself a teetotaler, heard a droning to his
left. A bright, large object flew by, stopped, and hovered just a few feet
over the park lawn.

According to O'Barski, the object or vehicle was circular and flat on the
bottom, with vertical sides and a convex roof. The vehicle was about eight
feet high and thirty feet across. O'Barski saw ten or twelve oblong, vertical windows spaced equally around the craft. Lights from inside the vehicle illuminated the area.

Then, as he watched, O'Barski said, a landing ladder came down, a door
opened, and eight to eleven figures, no more than three and a half feet tall,
descended. O'Barski said the figures wore jump suits and helmets and
seemed to be scooping up samples of soil and putting them into bags. Then
they climbed back into the UFO and quickly departed. The next day, in
daylight, O'Barski returned to the park and found a series of holes in the
ground, four or five inches wide and six inches deep.

There were to be many sightings of UFOs in this area over the next
month, but there were two other sightings that night that seemed to confirm the O'Barski testimony.

Incident 2: At about 9:30 P.M., January 11 — roughly five and one-half
hours before the O'Barski sighting — the Wamsleys, a North Bergen family
of five, reported seeing a domed UFO with oblong windows, giving off a
hum, pass near their house. It seemed to disappear near a large apartment
building called the Stonehenge.

Incident 3: At some time between 2:30 and 3:00 A.M., January 12 —
apparently just minutes before the O'Barski sighting — William Pawlowski
was on duty as the doorman at the Stonehenge. The apartment building
is directly across the street from North Hudson Park. Suddenly Pawlowski
saw a series of eight to fifteen bright, round lights attached to a dark, round
vehicle that was hovering over the park. Pawlowski did a double take and

then telephoned one of the tenants. While he was speaking, he heard a very high-pitched sound and saw the plate-glass lobby window crack near the floor. Glass was gouged out of the window from the street side.

Then the lights disappeared. The doorman estimated that any projectile or force that could clear the street wall and hit near the bottom of the window like that would have had to originate several feet above the level of the park.

Independently of one another, both the doorman Pawlowski and the motorist O'Barski picked out for UFO investigators the exact same spot for the hovering UFO.

Do UFOs exist? Go to the Stonehenge apartments and ask the tenants there if they believe in UFOs. Perhaps it would be simpler to tote up the numbers of those who don't believe!

We could call North Bergen, New Jersey, a "flap" area, and there are many more around the country. In fact, there is now a theory that there are three major flap areas in the United States, falling in three specific parts of the country. All are shaped more or less in the form of triangles. These areas, though slightly lopsided, indicate triangular boundaries which can be ascertained by using a pencil and ruler to mark the coordinates on a map. Roughly, they constitute the following:

Northwest: From a point near Seattle, Washington, through Idaho to a point near Great Falls, Montana; then through Wyoming to a point near Durango, Colorado; through Utah, Idaho, and Oregon to Seattle.

Southwest: Start at a point near Phoenix, Arizona; go through New Mexico and Texas to a point near Tulso, Oklahoma; then down to a point near Calvert, Texas; and finally back through New Mexico to Phoenix.

Midwest: From a point near Bismarck, North Dakota, through Minnesota, Iowa, and Wisconsin to a point near Grand Rapids, Michigan; continue through Indiana, Illinois, and Missouri to a point near Wichita, Kansas; go back through Nebraska and South Dakota to Bismarck, North Dakota.

Of course, these are not hard and fast boundaries, but there is no disputing that within these rough coordinates are rich UFO areas. For our purposes we can make a close study of any of the three. Let us consider the southwest triangle.

Of all the states lying wholly or partly within the triangle, Texas must be singled out for special attention as perhaps the most fascinating flap area. It appears that Texas has played host to more UFOs than any other section of the United States. Since 1947, according to many serious accounts, Texas has been zeroed in on by more than 5000 UFOs.

Let's narrow our study of the southwest triangle to one of its angles: Calvert, Texas, where two of the imaginary lines intersect. This town, about seventy-five miles northeast of Austin, has to qualify as the premier town for saucer-sighting statistics. Since 1956, well over two hundred UFO sightings have been made in and around Calvert.

Gracia Unger, editor of the *Calvert Tribune*, has stated: "More UFOs have been sighted here than probably anywhere else in the U.S.A." UFO activities reached a peak in Calvert in November and December of 1974, with 102 sightings in sixty days. Unger continued: "No one knows why the UFOs pick Calvert, but the strongest theory is because there is a big airbase here and several radar installations."

Some of the residents of Calvert who have actually seen UFOs include a number of respected citizens who don't exactly have a reputation for imagining things. In fact, many are trained observers; one is a deputy sheriff. Others are people of substance who have little or no reason to put themselves in a position to be ridiculed.

Here is the encounter experienced by a 36-year-old businessman who lives near Calvert:

"The thing stood there and looked at me for at least two and a half minutes. I was petrified with fear. I don't think I even blinked my eyes once, I was so scared. It was my day off and I was taking a hike through the woods, as I often do, when I saw the saucer. It was about six hundred yards away when I first spotted it; greenish-blue and reddish-purple in color and about twenty-five feet in diameter. There was a kind of dome with two windows on top, and it rested on four metal legs.

"I got to within about a hundred feet of the object when this, uh, well, thing stepped out from some bushes. It was about five feet tall and wore a silver, coverall-type suit and skin-tight mittens or gloves. It had some sort of protective helmet on, but it was transparent and I could see its weird face. The eyes were set wide apart and the chin came to a point.

"The creature walked toward me and stopped maybe ten or fifteen feet away from me. Then it pulled something from its right side, lifted it to its face and the object flashed. My guess is that it was probably some sort of camera. The object flashed again, and that's when I took off like a bat out of hell."

The man does not want to be identified for fear of being ridiculed in his business circles, but he is hardly the only Texan who has witnessed strange sights, especially around Calvert.

According to one newspaper report — not in the *Calvert Tribune* — a Washington source considered highly reliable has said, "The government is aware of the unusual number of UFO sightings in and around Calvert, Texas, and a discreet investigation is right now taking place. When all the facts have been gathered and carefully examined perhaps then we'll have some of the questions answered."

This Washington source also revealed that the investigators were especially interested in the "underwater aspect," obviously referring to a sighting made by editor Unger herself on November 21, 1973.

"For several nights we had received reports of a brightly colored, egg-shaped vessel over the Brazos River Bridge six miles east of Calvert. On this night, around seven o'clock, three others and I saw a UFO land on the river — and in a twinkling of an eye it submerged in the water, extinguishing all its lights in the process. We waited more than four hours but it did not reappear."

There are dozens of other reports by Calvertans, enough to make most of the citizens of Calvert believers.

Just ask television repairman and ham radio operator Virgil Chappel if he became a believer after his encounter.

"One night," Chappel related, "I glanced up in the sky and saw a radiating light maneuvering over the treetops. I grabbed a pair of binoculars — and saw the heavens dotted with a multitude of eerie-colored, pulsating lights of violet, red, yellow and blue hues. They were disc-shaped."

Billy R. Hall, a Calvert banker, described what he saw on November 15, 1973: "Through binoculars I could make out that the UFO was gun-metal gray and had a bubble-like structure on top. This was definitely a 'ship,' not a star or a flare."

A deputy sheriff, who asked not to be identified, said he observed a UFO for forty-five minutes during daylight. "It came so close," he said, "I could tell positively that it was not an aircraft."

Calvert grain store owner Steve Abraham and his 17-year-old daughter, Shirley, witnessed a UFO hovering above a tree one night as they were driving in their car.

"As we neared Fish Creek Bridge," Abraham reported, "we saw an image that resembled a bell, with a reddish-orange glow emanating from the bottom. After a few seconds the glow dimmed and seemed to go out. Then, just as suddenly, it came back on brighter than before. All at once, a very brilliant spotlight appeared.

"Then the UFO came down at a rapid speed toward the highway and over our car. I thought it was going to run over us, but as it got closer it turned upward and disappeared over the trees."

On June 27, 1974, Alice Tribble, a Calvert housewife, experienced a UFO encounter which she recounted to authorities: "I had just let my little dog out when I saw something hanging in the sky over our old oak tree. It was really weird. It was bluish-white and had a band of red lights around it. It was at least fifty feet across. After hovering in one spot for about fifteen minutes, it shot straight up — vanishing in space."

These are only a few of the Calvert sightings, but more than enough to make for a genuine flap area, and certainly enough to make this town a stopping point for UFO hunters.

There are many more such flap areas in the three big UFO triangles, and there are more elsewhere in the country, too.

People in Exeter, New Hampshire, experienced a prolonged rash of UFO encounters for several weeks. Policemen made sightings, housewives made sightings. The flap grew so intense that a leading reporter, John Fuller, launched a thorough investigation and wrote a landmark UFO book, *Incident at Exeter.*

Erie, Pennsylvania, was the site of a UFO flurry that lasted many months. After scores of sightings, researchers started calling Erie a "nesting ground" for UFOs.

Pompton Lakes, near Paterson, New Jersey, was another site of prolonged saucer activity. Many of the witnesses, including a number of policemen, were considered very reliable. Again and again over a two-year period, there were steady reports of brightly glowing objects "the size of an automobile" hovering in the skies.

Are all of these reports true? It is highly unlikely. Of course, many were faked, possibly in an attempt to "keep up with the Joneses." Others may well have been honest mistakes involving perfectly natural events. But a false alarm here doesn't make another report there automatically a fake.

The events in Pascagoula, Mississippi, are a case in point. A cab driver reported that while driving down Highway 90, he was startled by a blue light that came up behind his cab and then landed in his path. His engine stalled and his radio would not play. He said he realized something weird was going on, so he "ducked down in the seat." Then he heard a tapping sound on the window and looked up. Standing there was a strange creature with claws glaring down at him.

UFO researchers pressed him for more details. He couldn't give them. His story became tangled and then he confessed that he had fallen asleep in his cab and had made up the story to account for his time.

That UFO sighting in Pascagoula was a fake, but there was another sighting in that town by two fishermen, a confrontation that Ufologists regard as perhaps one of the most extensive encounters of the third kind. The sighting and actual physical encounter by 19-year-old Calvin Parker and 42-year-old Charles Hickson are described in Chapter 4 under the Mississippi entry. After a full discussion of the facts, readers can decide for themselves if Pascagoula should be regarded as a UFO hot spot.

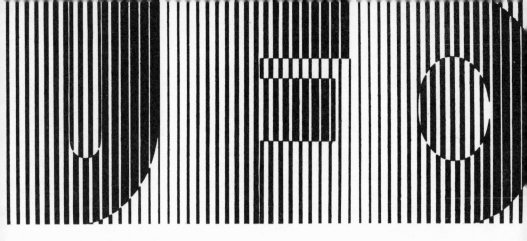

Chapter 4

UFOs IN DIXIE

Chapter 4
UFOs IN DIXIE

UFOs have a nasty habit of not abiding by borders, making it sometimes difficult to pinpoint all sightings on a state-by-state basis. Since this book is intended to be a specific geographical "travel guide," this leads to an occasional "oversweep" situation. We will at times speak of a phenomenon covering a very large area, sweeping from one state to another. For this reason, instead of listing the states alphabetically, we have grouped them by geographical areas.

We will start with the South. But wait a moment — are West Virginia are Maryland considered part of the South? Whose side did they fight on in the Civil War? They are not the South by political standards perhaps, but by UFO standards they are. The sightings experienced there are quite similar to those made in neighboring southern states.

So let us follow the UFO march through Dixie.

ALABAMA

HUNTSVILLE

Sightings in Alabama go back at least to 1910. Even that long ago, wide sweeps of UFOs were evident. A dispatch in the New York *Tribune* of January 13 of that year reads: "An airship passed over Chattanooga at great altitude at 9 o'clock this morning. Thousands saw the craft and heard the 'chugging' of the engine. Tonight a dispatch from Huntsville, Alabama, announced that the airship passed over the city travelling at a high speed."

This could not have been a "dirigible" flying from Chattanooga to Huntsville, a distance of seventy-five miles. At that time, a flight of seven or eight miles was considered quite remarkable. Either we are dealing with two dirigibles — not very likely — or one UFO.

Perhaps a clue is to be found in a news story that appeared in the same newspaper on the following day: "A white dirigible passed over Chattanooga at 11 o'clock this morning. It came from the South. A man was discernible in the machine. A mysterious airship was reported in southern Tennessee and northern Alabama last night."

MONTGOMERY

On July 24, 1948, an Eastern Airlines DC-3 was on its way from Houston, Texas, to Atlanta, Georgia. At about 2:45 A.M., the plane, flown by Captain Charles S. Chiles and John B. Whitted, was passing twenty miles southwest of Montgomery, Alabama. One report reads: "Chiles saw a light dead ahead and closing fast. His first reaction . . . was that it was a jet, but in an instant he realized that even a jet couldn't close as fast." As Chiles called it to the attention of co-pilot Whitted, the object moved into position "almost on top of them" Chiles banked the plane hard to the left and "as the UFO flashed by about 700 feet to the right, the DC-3 hit turbulent air. Whitted looked back just as the UFO pulled into a steep climb."

This incident occurred in the middle of the night while most of the passengers were asleep. However, one of them, Clarence L. McKelvie, a managing editor of the American Education Press, also observed the strange object. His later comments: "The male steward said to me, 'I noticed you watching out the window.' I told him there was something flashing — it looked like a cigar with a cherry flame going out the back. There was a row of windows and going in that direction fast. It made no noise. I heard nothing, because of the sound of the plane. It disappeared very quickly . . . It was on the right side of the plane, going off the horizon. It disappeared . . . or we went past it.

"The steward asked if I would talk to the pilot. Yes. The pilot came back and took down verbatim. He didn't say anything — he was shook. He said he had flown all during the war and 'this is the strangest experience I ever had.' He was shaking all the time.

"Oh, I was interrogated by groups — Air Force Intelligence of Wright-Patterson and Hynek's group. I was asked: 'Do you think it was a flying saucer?' I didn't know — I was looking at it on edge. If I had been looking above or below, but I was looking directly. Couldn't tell. Scared me to death . . . with the plane falling and seeing that thing go by. . . . It was hair-raising."

MOBILE

On November 14, 1956, Capt. W. J. Hull sighted a wildly maneuvering UFO while piloting a Capital Airlines flight sixty miles from Mobile. Both he and his co-pilot watched the strange craft execute chandelles (abrupt climbing turns), sudden stops, and "lazy eights." Then, suddenly, the UFO disappeared in a fantastic burst of speed.

ARKANSAS

BRINKLEY

Mrs. Ned Warnock of Brinkley was looking out her window on the night of March 8, 1967, when she spotted a flying object. "It was a reddish orange," she was quoted by the Monroe *County Sun*. "And it changed to a silver-white color just before it took off. It was round and pretty large. It was real low but gained height and speed as it took off. It was moving too fast for a star." Mrs. Warnock called a neighboring couple, Mr. and Mrs. J. H. Folkerts, and they also viewed the strange object.

FORT SMITH

During a great flap in the state on August 16, 1967, there were hundreds of sightings, concentrated along two belts running the length of the state from north to south. Remarkably, there were no sightings in neighboring states, which seems to rule out meteors or other natural phenomena. In Fort Smith, newsman John Garner took his Station KFSA microphone into the streets and broadcast a description of the strange, multicolored lights that veered over the city for hours while crowds of people watched.

BLYTHEVILLE AIR FORCE BASE

On October 21, 1967, an airman and two tower operators were on duty at the alert pad at the end of the runway of Blytheville Air Force Base when they saw what they described as "two oblong-shaped devices having the appearance of a table platter." Because the weather was clear and the visibility perfect, they were able to watch the objects for about half a minute. They could not determine what the objects were.

LITTLE ROCK, COLLIERSVILLE, BENTON, WEST HELENA, SHADY GROVE

Sightings were reported in all of these communities on October 4, 1973. Near Shady Grove, the sheriff's office recorded an account of "a very bright light moving up and down with a tail similar to a comet."

FLORIDA

HOLLYWOOD

Mr. and Mrs. Frank Burke of Hollywood reported seeing something like a rocket, with "flames at the bottom," during the evening of August 22, 1973. They watched from their backyard until the strange presence disappeared into the Everglades area about twenty-five miles away. The Burke sighting was confirmed by a number of pilots. A theory that the phenomenon was connected with the Kennedy Space Center was held until it was announced that there had been no launchings at the Center during the period in question.

PATRICK AIR FORCE BASE

Two weather specialist officers and several other persons watched four yellowish lights move around on the perimeter of Patrick Air Force Base on August 10, 1962.

WEST PALM BEACH INTERNATIONAL AIRPORT

Early on the morning of September 14, 1972, a strange flying object appeared at the West Palm Beach International Airport. It was tracked by two air traffic controllers, C. J. Fox and A. W. Brown. "It was like nothing I've ever seen," Brown reported.

Through binoculars, Federal Aviation Agency supervisor George Morales watched the unknown machine, unlike any aircraft. It was elliptical and cigar-shaped. Another report of the same object came in from Eastern Airlines Captain B. F. Ferguson. Then the UFO was reported by state and city police and many private citizens. Now FAA operators at Miami International Airport and radarmen at Homestead Air Force Base started tracking it. On orders from NORAD, the North American Air Defense Command, two F-106 interceptors were scrambled at Homestead at 6:00 A.M. One of the pilots, Maj. Gerald Smith, climbed above the clouds and spotted the glowing UFO. As he tried to close in, it disappeared.

Attempts were made to ascribe the glowing UFO to the planet Venus. This, however, conflicted with the FAA controllers' records. Their radar had tracked a hard, solid "target" less than sixteen miles away. The visual reports confirmed that estimate.

SEBRING

On September 20, 1966, J. J. O'Connor, a Florida lawyer and former Army security investigator, was flying in his private plane near Sebring. At 9500 feet a UFO — so large that its shadow covered O'Connor's plane — came down directly above him. O'Connor, taking evasive action, reduced power and dived. Pulling out at 3500 feet, he discovered the object had come down with him. Now truly worried, he reached for a .38 revolver he kept in his cockpit. He decided that the object was too big for the weapon to have any effect. After a few more chilling moments, the UFO moved upward and disappeared.

GEORGIA

GRIFFIN

Close encounters with UFOs frequently lead to observers finding physical traces of the phenomenon after it has departed. There are often changes in vegetation or soil and sometimes damage to property. On September 10, 1973, witnesses in Griffin reported that an egg-shaped object had landed in a field. Several hours after their report, soil in a depression found in the field still measured 200 to 300 F.

ALBANY

On August 30, 1973, a year-long spate of aerial aliens sweeping Georgia came to a head in Albany. Other communities reporting sightings were Adel, Ashburn, Camilla, Cordele, Dawson, Doe Run, Dougherty County, Leesburg, Macon, Moultrie, Pelham, Vienna, Waycross, Sandersville, and Tifton. State trooper A. L. Cahill, together with Sergeant Jerry Crawley and Office John Harris of the Americus Police Department, saw strange objects pass in the sky over Dawson toward Albany.

"It was a real bright white light traveling in the sky . . . rather large," Cahill reported. A patrolman in Leesburg stated that "the object is round, with orange, red, green and blue lights." In Camilla, a half dozen persons watched a "display" that lasted three and a half hours. "It looks like a white light with blinking green and red lights," one witness reported. "It has moved in a zigzag pattern and then moved slowly to the west." In Sandersville, announcer Ray Smith of Station WSNT reported twelve different colored lights after listeners alerted him by calling his program. Smith said, "We've seen about ten or twelve of these things. They're generally blue in color but change into red and sometimes green. They're smaller than stars and change colors, kind of like a kid's top."

Over a period of forty-eight hours, Robins Air Force Base (in the flap area) was deluged with calls. However, according to one reporter, base officials "did not record the calls because the Air Force does not admit the existence of UFOs." In Macon, Officer Dennis Brown disputed the claim that the hundreds of objects sighted were merely satellites and other debris. "I'll go against any man who says these things are a planet or scrap metal falling from space," he said. He had viewed four such objects through a ten-power rifle scope. "I believe the yellow or white lights are from the propulsion system. There is something inside. I believe the American government is experimenting with something and they don't want us to know about it."

GAINESVILLE - LAVONIA

On June 29, 1964, just before midnight, an amber-colored object flew

over the car of B. E. Parham of Wellford, South Carolina, on Route 59.
The object made a leap in the air above the vehicle and came back twice,
as though it was observing the headlights of Parham's car. The object
made "as much noise as a million hissing snakes" and left an odor of embalming fluid. The driver described the object as about the size of the
car, six feet high and spinning. Attached to the outer edges were some
devices that seemed to be antennae. There was a yellow light shining
through some openings in the lower part of the object. The heat was tremendous. After a two-mile chase, Parham stopped the car and turned
off the headlights. The object then rose into the sky and disappeared.

This particular encounter has proven to be of great interest to Ufologists Jacques and Janine Vallee since they uncovered a 1957 case in Vin-
sur-Caramy, France, with much the same characteristics. They doubt
rather strongly that the details of the French case were ever made known
to the citizens of Wellford, South Carolina.

TALLULAH FALLS

The week after the Parham sighting, a similar report was made in Tallulah
Falls by nine witnesses in three different houses. J. Ivester reported that
his television set started going haywire and he found it impossible to
watch, so he and his family went out for a breath of fresh air at 9:00 P.M.
They saw a flying object come just over the trees to within a few hundred
yards of the house. They thought it stopped over the garden of a neigh-
bor. The object was silent and only the lower part was very visible. They
saw three lights, red, white, and red, in a row. When the object started to
turn right, the three lights were no longer visible and a powerful green light
appeared which cast an eerie light over the countryside. They noticed an
odor of "brake liquid" or "embalming fluid." When Habersham County
Sheriff A. J. Chapman arrived at the scene a few minutes later, he could
still notice the strange smell.

KENTUCKY

WALLINGFORD

Following a 1951 UFO visitation to Wallingford, soil analysis of the site
revealed levels of chromium, iron, and manganese not normally found in
the clay soil of the area.

KELLY - HOPKINSVILLE

On August 21, 1965, there occurred what has been called the "granddaddy of all occupant sightings." A member of the Sutton family saw a light land in a gully near the family's farmhouse. He told others what he had seen and was subjected to considerable ridicule. Within a few minutes, however, a small "glowing" figure was seen approaching the house. Every member of the Sutton family — eleven in all — later described it as about three and a half feet tall, with a roundish head, elephantlike ears, huge eyes, a slitlike mouth, and long arms ending in clawlike hands.

The family dealt with the matter in characteristic backwoods style, firing several shots at it. The strange creature hurried off, but before long several more appeared. They were near the window, on the roof, and in the trees. The Suttons fired again and then went outside to see if they had killed the eerie intruder. When they got outside, the first man was passing under the roof overhang when a clawlike hand reached down and touched his hair. The Suttons cut loose again, both at the creature on the roof and at another one in a nearby tree. Although they seemed to be hit, the creatures just floated down and ran away.

Petrified, the family returned to the house and locked themselves in while the creatures cavorted outside for the next three hours. Finally, unable to take it any more, the entire family rushed to their cars and drove to the police station. The police returned with them but found nothing. After they left, the creatures reappeared and carried on their antics until dawn.

Depending on your outlook, this is either one of the most amazing or most preposterous of all UFO encounters. However, it seems strange that eleven members of one family would all take part in a hoax, especially since they have refused most interviews and never sought any financial remuneration. The Suttons also had a reputation for being a no-nonsense family.

Not surprisingly, the Kelly-Hopkinsville sighting area has long since been a stopping point for UFO tourists. Shortly after the sighting, traffic was piled up in both directions for half a mile. The attraction for the strange encounter remains because of strong feelings by many that it really did happen. The case was even listed in official Blue Book files as "Unidentified."

LOUISIANA

WATSON

From the Baton Rouge, Louisiana, *State Times*, October 19, 1973:

"Reports of UFO sightings in this area continued today — this time from Watson and Zachary.

"R. E. Clark said that he saw an object that emitted swirling vapor trails in much the same manner as a jet, only circular in shape. 'The vapor would swirl up in a circle, straighten out and then go up in a circle again,' he said, adding that the sightings occurred at 6:30 A.M. today and were also seen by fellow workers at a Baton Rouge grocery, some 15 miles away.

" 'I thought I was crazy,' Clark said, 'but the butchers at the store saw it, too. We can't all be going crazy.' "

ZACHARY

In the same issue of the *State Times*, the community of Zachary was reported to have had a different sort of encounter:

"In the other report, 'angel hair,' a long, white, silky substance that occasionally accompanies claims of UFO sightings, has been reported by a Zachary woman who said that two strings, about six feet in length, fell on her seven-year-old son yesterday.

"The filmy, string-like substances were like the threads of spiderwebs, sometimes five to six feet in length. They were reported at Shreveport, at Springhill, and 60 miles away at Ruston, as well as Zachary."

MARYLAND

LAUREL

On March 8, 1967, a police officer and two residents of Laurel watched an object that appeared to be circular and had "a shiny gold bottom" When it hovered, they reported, the top glowed red. It followed an oval-shaped path, moving back and forth from Laurel to Fort Meade three times before finally taking off.

LOCH RAVEN DAM

At 10:30 P.M. on October 26, 1958, two men were taking a Sunday drive toward the Loch Raven Reservoir near Baltimore. It was extremely dark but visibility was clear and there were constellations in the sky. As they rounded a bend on Loch Raven Boulevard, they came upon an egg-shaped object hovering over Bridge Number 1. It was hanging 100 to 150 feet from the top of the superstructure. They first saw the object from about three hundred yards away. They had been driving twenty to thirty miles per hour, which was somewhat fast since this was a bad road, and they slowed to ten or twelve miles per hour and came to within eighty feet of the object. Suddenly, the electrical system of the car gave out, as though someone had suddenly removed the battery. The driver tried to turn on the ignition but it was dead. Instead, he put on the brakes and he and his friend just sat and stared at the object. Then, one of the witnesses said, "We decided to run out of the car and we decided to put the car between ourselves and the object. It was a very narrow road: on one side the lake, and on the other side a cliff. There was no place to run. We probably would have if we could've, but we were terrified at what we saw.

"We thought maybe it was a Navy blimp. We tried to rationalize what it was. Of course, the fact that the electrical system in our car conked out made us a little suspicious as to what it might have been. . . .

"Although we are not sure, we estimate it was approximately one hundred feet long since it occupied approximately one-third of the bridge, at the height it was at. We watched it for approximately thirty seconds and then it seemingly gave off a terrific bright light.

"It had been glowing with an iridescent glow beforehand, but this light seemingly was blinding and approximately at the same time we felt a tremendous heat wave. It didn't seem like the heat of a burning object but something like an ultra-violet light or some kind of radiation. . . .

"The object disappeared from view within approximately five or ten seconds after giving off a tremendous thunder clap, something approaching a plane breaking the sound barrier. After it disappeared from sight we came back into the car and turned the ignition system on and it immediately went into operation."

The experience of these two men was partially confirmed by several other witnesses who reported seeing a strange light in the vicinity of the bridge.

MISSISSIPPI

PASCAGOULA

This community was the scene of the fake report of a UFO by the cab driver who fell asleep on the job. It was also the site of a "strange encounter of the third kind" — one which has proven very difficult to dismiss as a hoax.

On October 11, 1973, Charles Hickson, 42, and Calvin Parker, 19, were fishing in the quiet Pascagoula River when they were startled by a strange buzzing sound. They saw an egg-shaped object about ten feet wide and eight feet high. As it hovered just above the ground nearby, a door opened and several strange figures or humanoids "floated" down. Hickson and Parker later described them as being about five feet tall with bullet-shaped heads, light gray, wrinkled skin, slitlike mouths, no necks or eyes, clawlike hands, and conical appendages where humans have ears and noses.

Two of the creature-intruders seized the older man, Hickson, and "floated" him back into the UFO. Hickson was taken into a brightly lit room. In the meantime another creature had grabbed Parker, who then fainted. Hickson was held while a strange object resembling an eye moved over his body, apparently performing an examination. As far as the shocked man could tell, this "instrument" did not appear to be attached to anything. Hickson felt himself suspended in midair. He could move nothing except his eyes. After about twenty minutes, Hickson was floated back outside where he joined the hysterical Parker. The UFO then took off, straight up, and vanished.

The pair reported the incident to the sheriff, who was quite logically suspicious. They were left in a sound-monitored room and their conversations indicated they had not made up their story. The two men were also subjected to lie detector tests and both passed. Other probes by experts showed no evidence of a hoax. Hypnosis was attempted but proved too traumatic for the men.

TUPELO

Thomas E. Westmoreland, a National Park Service ranger, reported seeing a UFO in Tupelo on October 4, 1973. It was the size of a house, barely moving in the sky as it pulsated red, green, and yellow. He declared: "I've been dealing with the public for years and I know people exaggerate and see what they want to see, but I know I saw this."

HELL CREEK BOTTOM

On the same day as the Tupelo sighting, Sheriff's Deputy Irwin Carroll of Hell Creek Bottom was summoned by the Ollie Berry family and was able to confirm their sighting of an unknown object "like a quarter moon but five times as big." Mrs. Berry's daughter had viewed the phenomenon the longest and gave the most complete description, saying it was "first like a star, but longer. Then like a half moon. Then like a kite with a lot of red lights on its tail. Then it got round. Then it divided into three parts."

NORTH CAROLINA

GREENSBORO

There have been very frequent UFO sightings on military, weather bureau, and airport radar in Greensboro. Quite often, they were confirmed by witnesses on the ground. When the Federal Aviation Agency tower at the Greensboro-High Point Airport in Greensboro, North Carolina, showed an unidentified flying object on July 27, 1966, several police officers in the High Point-Randolph County area also reported seeing UFOs buzzing the area. According to these witnesses, the objects appeared to be at an altitude of five hundred feet and were described as round, brilliant red-green, and giving off flashes of light.

SOUTH CAROLINA

CHEROKEE COUNTY

In January and February of 1973, Cherokee County had a real flap with sightings in various communities including Beaverdam, Cashion Crossroads, Asbury-Rehoboth, Corinth, White Plains, Macedonia, and Draytonville. Among the various types of UFOs was a group of four red and yellow objects sailing in a pattern; a spherical apparition which appeared to be spinning on its own axis; a large ovoid which was accompanied by three cylindrical scouts; a luminescent, star-white triangular shape; and a shining object with windows and antennae. In this period hundreds of persons, including law officers, saw these UFOs. Often the witnesses were in groups of several people who all agreed on what they had seen.

TENNESSEE

BRUCEVILLE

On October 2, 1973, Otis West of Newbern, Tennessee, commander of the Dyer County Civil Air Patrol, and Doug Viar of VTRO radio station flew to Bruceville to chase some of the UFOs being reported in the area. West and Viar viewed an object which had three lights, one red, one green, and one white flashing light. As described by West, the UFOs were "landing out there in this field. They would come up from behind the trees and they would look like an orange ball. When they got up you could see the strobe flashing. They are spasmatic. They'll move real fast straight up and then they'll stop and they'll go left or right."

VIRGINIA

BRANDS FLAT

At 6:15 P.M. on January 19, 1965, an industrial worker in Brands Flat spotted two circular flying objects hovering at a low altitude over an archery range. The smaller of the two UFOs, about twenty feet in diameter, landed about eighteen yards from the man, and three creatures, about forty inches tall, came out. According to the witness, they uttered unintelligible sounds and then got back into the craft and flew away.

WILLIAMSBURG

In what has been described as an "incredible tale told by a credible witness," a businessman anxious to keep his name out of the papers because of his professional status reported to police that at 8:30 A.M. on January 23, 1965, he was driving near the intersection of U.S. Highway 60 and State Route 614 when his late-model Cadillac suddenly stalled. He then noticed an object hovering over a nearby field, only four feet from the ground. About eighty feet in height, twenty-five feet in diameter at the top, and ten feet in diameter at the bottom, it looked very much like a huge light bulb. The object was metallic gray and glowed red-orange on one side and blue on the other. The object made a whirring sound, like that of a vacuum cleaner.

Inside his stalled car, the businessman continued to observe the object as it hovered until finally, in a "rapid vanishing maneuver," it moved off horizontally. When it disappeared, the shaken businessman got out of his car and went back to another car which apparently had stalled behind him. He asked that driver if he had seen the object. He had.

This sighting troubled Blue Book a great deal and remained classified as "Unidentified." All sorts of explanations were offered: that the object was a low-altitude temperature inversion, a reflection of the sun, an ascending weather balloon, or low clouds combining to form a mirage. None seemed too likely — and would not explain the stalled cars.

HAMPTON

Two days after the Williamsburg sighting above, a strange craft came down near Hampton. Among the witnesses were two NASA research engineers, Major John Nayadley, a retired Air Force jet pilot, and A. G. Crimmins. "I watched it through binoculars," Crimmins said. "It was zigzagging as if searching for a landing spot. I could see flashing lights on the edge or rim of a rapidly rotating disc." After the UFO touched ground, it climbed steeply out of sight.

When questioned about the report, Air Force Headquarters put out the explanation that the craft had been a helicopter. As though NASA engineers could be rattled by a helicopter! Unfortunately, Langley Air Force Base killed this theory when it reported that no helicopters were flying in the area at that time.

MARION

On January 25, 1965, several persons, including a policeman, saw an object ascend from a wooded area on a hill. Inspection of the wooded area revealed some unusual markings on the ground.

WEST VIRGINIA

CHARLESTON

The big knock that UFO detractors have about sightings of UFOs by pilots is, they claim, that pilots lack the scholarly expertise of astronomers and can be fooled by phenomena that a trained scientist would fathom immediately. For instance, the theory holds, a scientist would not be misled by atmospheric conditions, clouds, planets, or stars.

A sighting that should satisfy such objections was made by the late Percy Wilkins, who was among the premier astronomers and perhaps the greatest selenographer.* On June 11, 1954, the English scientist was flying from Charleston, West Virginia, to Atlanta, Georgia. Looking out his window at about 10:45·A.M., Dr. Wilkins saw a cluster of cumulus clouds a couple of miles away — and right above them he saw two radiant ovoids. His recollection of them: "They looked exactly like polished metal dinner plates reflecting the sunlight as they flipped and banked around beside the clouds. Presently a third object came slowly out of a huge cloud, remaining motionless in the shadow of the cloud and therefore darker than the others. Presently it zipped away and plunged into another cloud mass. After about two minutes, the first two did the same maneuver and I did not see them again."

Judging by the estimated distance between the clouds and his plane and the seeming size of the objects — about the radius of the moon — the great astronomer calculated the diameter of the unknown objects to be almost fifty feet.

*Selenography is the science of the physical features of the moon.

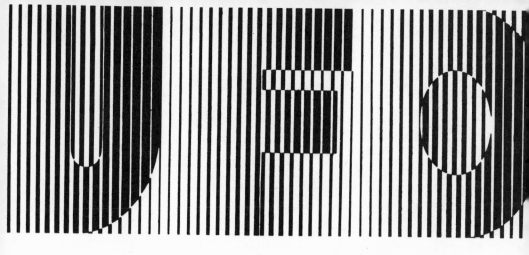

Chapter 5

THE CROWDED SOUTHWEST

Chapter 5

THE CROWDED SOUTHWEST

Dr. J. Allen Hynek, who became a believer after serving as a consultant to U.S. Air Force Project Blue Book, has stated that "one of the chief characteristics of UFO sightings seems to be their isolation in time and space. This is, of course, a highly puzzling feature and has contributed greatly to attempts to discredit the phenomenon."

UFOs clearly like to go where a lot of people aren't. This is one reason there are not generally a great number of witnesses to most incidents. It also explains why so many sightings occur in the wide-open Southwest — and why the encounters there tend to be most startling.

ARIZONA

SNOWFLAKE

Shocking — and controversial — is the encounter of Travis Walton in Snowflake, Arizona. On November 5, 1975, 23-year-old Walton was part of a seven-man lumbering crew riding in a truck. The men made a daylight sighting of a saucerlike object in the air about thirty yards from the road. The truck stopped and Walton decided to approach the object, which was making a "high-pitched, buzzing" sound. Then the strange object started to move. Walton stopped and crouched down by a log. Suddenly a beam came out of the bottom of the saucer and hit Walton, throwing the lumberman about ten feet, according to the estimate of one witness. Walton himself reported that he had "felt a kind of electric shock [which] knocked me out." The rest of the crew was terrified and drove off in the truck "as fast as we could."

Walton disappeared after that. A sheriff's posse looked for him for five days without success. Then Walton called relatives from a highway phone booth. He told his relatives that he believed he had been in the UFO during that entire time, but he said he had been awake no more than a few hours in that period. He said he awoke in an all-metal room, which struck him as a hospital. His shirt was pulled up, and a "thing," not attached to anything, was across his chest. There were three "aliens" with him. All were about five feet tall and bald, with chalky white skin. They had generally small features except for large brown eyes. They were dressed in "orangeish-brown coveralls." Walton created a disturbance, knocking the "thing" off his chest and pushing away the aliens. They left the room without saying a word. Then another person entered the room; at least Walton described him as "human." He was six feet tall and had brownish-blond hair and golden-hazel eyes. He wore a blue uniform and a "clear, bubble-type helmet."

This "human" merely smiled at Walton's babbling and led him to a smaller room down a hallway, where three other "humans" placed a clear, soft, form-fitting plastic mask over his face. The mask had a black ball attached to it, "like an oxygen mask," but it had no tubes. Walton then passed out and remembered nothing else until he woke up on the roadway in time to see "this craft disappear straight up."

A weekly newspaper, the *National Enquirer*, awarded Walton and the witnesses $5000 for their account of the experience, but needless to say, the Walton story has been the subject of considerable controversy. One well-known UFO skeptic, Philip Klass, came up with documentary evidence that Walton had been subjected to a secret lie detector test five days after his return and had flunked it. Klass charged that a hoax was set up to end a government lumbering contract. The lumber crew chief, himself one of the witnesses, held a contract which was not being completed on time. However, if the contract was cancelled, he stood to collect about $2000 in withheld Forest Service funds. It was cancelled.

Walton's supporters are not impressed with this, nor are they upset that Walton failed the lie detector test. They point out that he was suffering a continuing emotional upset over his experience and was in no shape for the test. Perhaps more important is that if the lie detector criteria is so important in the Walton story, what about the Pascagoula, Mississippi, case where a lie detector *supported* the story of a UFO close encounter?

NEW MEXICO

SOCORRO

This is the site of what is regarded as a UFO classic. Numerous efforts have been made to discredit this sighting, without any real success. The best that some commercial debunkers have been able to come up with is that it is all a "town plot" to entice more tourists to Socorro. There is no doubt that Socorro deserves more tourists — the sighting there has never been disproved or the main story shaken to any degree.

At about 5:45 P.M. on April 24, 1964, Lonnie Zamora, a local police-man, was chasing a speeder when he saw a bluish-white flame and an ob-ject dropping in altitude over the desert about three quarters of a mile away. Zamora forgot about the speeder; he was more concerned about the fact that there was a dynamite shack nearby that could be caused to explode. He veered off into the desert and drove up a steep hill. Look-ing down from the hill, he saw a white or silvery egg-shaped object in a gully about two hundred yards away. It was supported by four unequal legs, and next to it were two figures. They were "either large kids or small adults." The figures were dressed in white coveralls and "seemed startled" by Zamora's presence.

Zamora got out of his car to work his way around the hill to get a clos-er look. He temporarily lost sight of the object and heard a bang. When he came in view of the object again, he discovered that the two figures had disappeared. Then the craft took off with a thunderous roar. Zam-ora was able to make out some sort of red insignia on the craft. The UFO headed southeast, moving on a straight line off the ground for ten to fif-teen miles. It cleared a nearby river mouth and, without smoke, flames, or noise, simply went away.

Policemen who answered Zamora's emergency call were the first to reach the scene. They went down into the gully and discovered deep marks in the ground. FBI and Air Force witnesses joined the investigat-ing team and found bent and burned brush in several places. They meas-ured the distance between four indentations in the sand which formed a quadrilateral whose diagonals intersected at a right angle. The mid-points of the quadrilateral would contain a circle; logically, the center of the circle would be directly under the vehicle's center of gravity. The main fire scar was found at that spot.

The investigators reached some definite conclusions: They had no doubt that Zamora did not lie. He did not suffer a hallucination. Some-thing had most definitely landed there. There were traces of calcination, but spectroscopic analysis of the calcined area proved negative, and the mode of propulsion appeared radically different from any craft of Amer-ican construction.

UFO supporters look to the Socorro case as prime evidence of UFOs. They point out that the indentations were not similar to any such mark-ings in the surrounding area. They regard talk of the Socorro encounter as a hoax or a hallucination to be a contrived solution itself. There is, says Dr. Hynek, "much more evidence to indicate that we are dealing with a most real phenomenon of undetermined origin."

OKLAHOMA

BOWLEN SPRINGS

In February of 1974, Clay Knight, who owns a dairy farm near Bowlen Springs, Oklahoma, saw a silver-colored, shiny unidentified flying object that seemed to be taking off from his pasture when he first spotted it about 4:30 A.M. Sheriff's Deputy Joe Davenport said the farmer described the mysterious object as having flashing red and orange lights and being as big as a bedroom. "He said it was making a high-pitched noise, real shrill. His herd dog got so scared from the flashing lights and noise that he took off to the house or garage or somewhere and he never could get him to come out again."

The witness also exhibited a trait that is becoming more and more common to viewers of UFOs. According to the deputy, "I never saw a man that was so anxious to prove what he said he had seen. It was absolutely fascinating how bad he wanted me to know that he wasn't telling a wild story that wasn't true. I don't have any reason not to believe him. He's a college graduate and obviously a man of high intelligence."

HENRYETTA

At 8:45 P.M. on March 8, 1967, Mrs. Homer Smith of Henryetta walked out onto her back porch and "was astonished to see a twirling object with colored lights" going over Ninth Street and heading south. Mrs. Smith called her 10-year-old son, and he too saw the strange sight. The woman said the UFO was traveling and twirling so fast that it was very difficult to count the lights on it. She said they were colored and she believed the rear of the ship had what looked like "spits of fire coming from it."

TEXAS

HOUSTON

"Angel's hair" has intrigued UFO investigators for many years. It is a fibrous, weblike substance that covers the ground, trees, and other areas in amounts believed too large to be attributed to spiders. The material usually disintegrates quite rapidly, but in some cases it has lasted long enough to be analyzed. Very often the material has been seen descending from a UFO or found in an area where a UFO has been reported. Such material was found to have fallen near Houston on November 6, 1968, during a UFO sighting. According to a report in the Houston *Post*, the substance "would not dissolve in water, alcohol or sulfuric acid. . . . Microscopic and tactile examination indicates the substance is fibrous, elastic, relatively strong, somewhat sticky, and white in color."

LEVELLAND

The premier Texas UFO encounter began in Levelland, a town in the Texas Panhandle, on November 2, 1957. The most startling aspect was the number of reports made, independent of one another, over a very short period of time.

Patrolman A. J. Fowler was the duty officer when the first call came in shortly after 11:00 P.M. Two men, Pedro Saucedo and Joe Salaz, were driving in a truck four miles west of town when they saw an illuminated object hurtling rapidly toward their car. Saucedo's later certified statement reads: "To whom it may concern: on the date of November 2, 1957 I was traveling north and west on route 116, driving my truck. At about four miles out of Levelland, I saw a big flame, to my right front ... I thought it was lightning. But when this object had reached to my position it was different, because it put my truck motor out and lights. Then I stopped, got out, and took a look, but it was so rapid and quite some heat that I had to hit the ground. It also had colors — yellow, white — and looked like a torpedo, about 200 feet long, moving at about 600 to 800 miles an hour."

Officer Fowler's first inclination was to put down Saucedo's report as the case of a drunk seeing things, but as matters developed it would appear that the town of Levelland was on its biggest mass drunk in history. Fowler got another call from a driver on the opposite side of town who said he had come upon a brilliantly lit egg-shaped object, about two hundred feet long, sitting in the middle of the road. The driver's car engine and headlights then failed. He got out of his car and the egg-shaped vehicle promptly rose some two hundred feet, hovered a moment, and then disappeared. The driver got back into his car and was surprised to discover that he was able to restart his engine. All in all, Fowler received no less than fifteen phone calls giving similar details and experiences.

Fowler reported the events to his superiors, and Sheriff Weir Clem and Deputy Pat McCulloch went out to patrol the roads. Meanwhile more calls were coming in. Then, at 1:30 A.M., Sheriff Clem and Deputy McCulloch, while cruising on Oklahoma Flat Road about four miles out of town, spotted an enormous egg of light "looking like a brilliant red sunset across the highway." The object appeared to be about a thousand feet from them and "lit up the whole pavement in front of us for about two seconds." The only thing different about the Clem-McCulloch sightings and most of the others is that they reported no interference with their car's electrical system.

The following day there were more incidents and sightings stretching from that area of Texas on into New Mexico.

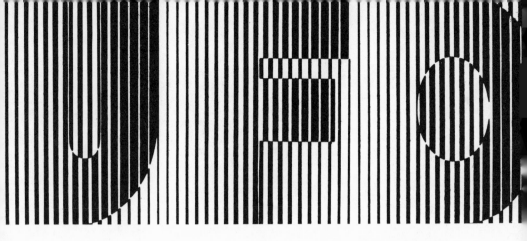

Chapter 6

THE MIDWEST

Chapter 6
THE MIDWEST

ILLINOIS

PONTIAC

Early in March, 1967, many witnesses in Pontiac reported sightings to the Illinois State Police. All said they had seen a white light flash from time to time with a red light and a periodic green light. The object appeared from about 10:00 P.M. to midnight and moved slowly up and down. "More than a dozen people have seen the object this week," the Pontiac *Leader* reported.

KNOX COUNTY

Deputy Sheriff Frank Courson was among the twenty-odd people in Knox County who watched a pulsating red and white circular object for several hours on the night of March 8, 1967. According to the general description, the object looked like an upside-down bowl and was about two thousand feet from the ground. In an interesting fillip, Deputy Courson added that "a similar object" crossed his car on Monday as he drove along Interstate 74 near Galesburg, but he "was scared to tell anyone about it then."

LITTLETON

At 4:45 A.M. on July 20, 1964, an Illinois state employee was driving on Route 101 about four miles west of Littleton when he caught sight of an object rising above the treetops, just in the process of taking off. The ob-

An engraving that appeared in the San Francisco *Call* in 1896, depicting the famous "Airship" of 1896-97 that apparently crossed the continent, first appearing in California and last being sighted in Yonkers, New York.

ject had the shape of a half-sphere. He immediately judged it to be a rocket of some kind and thought to himself that the fuel mixture was too rich because the jets seemed to be purple-red in color. Then he realized that what he first considered "jets" were really formed by a luminous cone that opened beneath the object. This cone had made the object appear to be rising on flames. The object rose higher in the sky and then turned and faced the man. It stayed there for just a few seconds and then turned again, climbed in the sky, and vanished.

INDIANA

PORTLAND

Indiana has long been a leading state for UFO sightings. Portland is the site of one of the most credible reports in the saga of the Great Airship sightings of 1896-1897. Reports started on the west coast and moved east until the final sighting in Yonkers, New York, on April 30, 1897. Such publications as *Scientific American* dismissed the sightings as "creations from the brains of imaginative persons."

The best description of the strange ship, and one considered in Indiana to be from a totally reliable source, was made by a Presbyterian minister in Portland. He described seeing an "aerodrome" consisting of parallel fuselages, one over the other, with movable fins and swirling fans, giving the appearance of a turbine-driven craft.

IOWA

CLINTON

Fifteen minutes after the sighting near Littleton, Illinois, described on page 73, an Air Force man driving near Clinton saw a strange light in the sky. He stopped his car and listened but heard no noise coming from the object, which was moving north-northwest. He was able to watch the object for a full minute until it disappeared. The airman described it as a large cone, very bright on top, but more diffuse towards the base, which blended with the background of the sky.

ELDORA

The Eldora *Herald-Ledger* of March 14, 1967, reported: "On Wednesday,

Thursday, and Friday nights of last week unidentified flying objects were reported by several persons . . . including Dr. and Mrs. W. G. Tietz, Connie Dagit and her younger brother, Jack Chadwick, and John Kiwala. The UFOs west of Eldora were all reported at approximately the same time nightly, at about 8:30 P.M. UFOs have also been reported in the Steamboat Rock area."

BOONE

Also in March of that year, Mrs. L. E. Koppenhaver reported seeing "a big red ball" sailing right over her house at 9:45 P.M. "You know how the setting sun gets a red glow on it?" she said. "Well, that was what this thing looked like. Only this object was very mobile, moving almost out of sight, the bright glow diminishing to a small light. I've seen satellites before, but this was nothing like them. It moved so fast and maneuvered so quickly." Her father, Walter Engstrom, also witnessed the event.

MICHIGAN

DETROIT

On March 8, 1967,* police received eight reports of a UFO hovering over Liggett School in Detroit at about 8:00 P.M. The Air Force and the Grosse Point Woods police investigated reports of a "burning orange oval" which had been photographed by two persons. Maj. Raymond Nyls, Selfridge Air Force Base operations officer, was quoted as saying, "There was definitely something out there. Too many people saw it."

DEXTER

This was the scene of the famous Michigan "swamp gas" UFOs. On March 14, 1966, Deputy Sheriffs J. Foster and B. Bushroe observed several disc-shaped objects maneuvering above Dexter. Then they spotted four UFOs flying in line formation. Three other police agencies joined in with reports and Selfridge Air Force Base confirmed with radar tracking. In an

---

*Readers will note that the date of March 8, 1967, turns up very often. In fact, it is a most remarkable date in UFO history: no less than twenty-two UFO sightings were made in various parts of the country on that particular Wednesday.

Photo taken by three men in Pontiac, Michigan, who said they saw two flying discs in the evening sky.

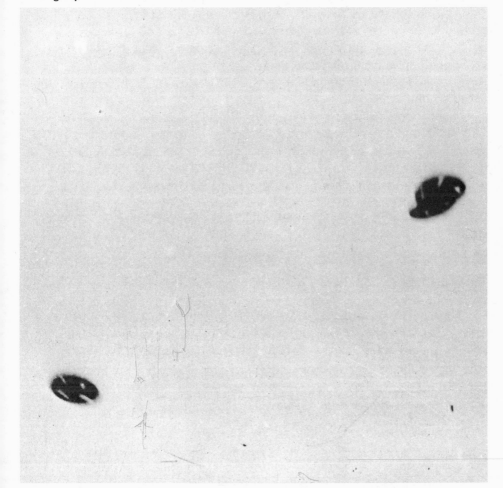

official report, Deputy Bushroe said, "This is the strangest thing that Deputy Foster and myself have ever witnessed. . . . These objects could move at fantastic speeds, and make very sharp turns, dive and climb, and hover, with great maneuverability."

Six days later, on March 20, two or three lights were reported moving around in a swamp outside Dexter. The same sort of lights were reported the next night in Hillsdale, Michigan. The Dexter sightings became top news. The then House Minority Leader Gerald Ford demanded a congressional investigation. Trying to cool things, the Air Force sent Dr. Hynek, still at that stage a disbeliever, to Michigan. He had barely begun his investigation when the Air Force ordered him to hold a press conference and debunk the reports. By that time there were also reports of more flying objects with high-speed maneuverability. Unable to come up with any explanation for the high-flying UFOs, Dr. Hynek tried to focus on the ground light reports. Without being very definite, he told reporters it was possible that marsh gas, caused by decaying vegetable matter in swampy areas, could have been the cause of the sightings. Before Hynek could finish, reporters dashed to the telephones and the swamp gas theory was published around the world.

The Air Force took a terrible roasting for such a stupid explanation. The Richmond *News Leader* urged the Air Force to stop suppressing evidence and trying to discredit witnesses. The South Bend *Tribune* headlined: "AIR FORCE INSULTS PUBLIC WITH SWAMP GAS THEORY."

To this day there has been no solid explanation of the Dexter UFOs.

MINNESOTA

FLOODWOOD

From the Floodwood *Rural Forum* of March 9, 1967: "A strange object in the sky hovering above our homes here is giving some of us folks the shivers. It's becoming such a mysterious light or flying saucer that we can almost work our imaginations into seeing it land some green men from outer space into our backyard. The thing moves with a gliding motion with brilliant light and sometimes just hovering and sometimes moving with utmost speed. It appears each night at 8 o'clock and stays for about one hour before it fades away."

LONG PRAIRIE

A very close encounter of the third kind occurred in Long Prairie, a small community west of Minneapolis, on October 23, 1965. It happened to a radio announcer with an impeccable reputation. His own narrative follows:

"I was driving west on Minnesota Highway 27 when I went around a bend in the road and my car engine stopped running and my lights went off. I looked up and saw this object standing in the middle of the road. It was around 7:15 P.M. . . . I had just checked my watch a minute before, so I know what time it was. I finally coasted to a stop about twenty feet from it. . . . I tried to start my car but it would not start. I did not get any response to my starter. I then got out of my car with the idea to go up to it and try to rock the center of gravity and topple it over so that I would have the evidence right there in black and white. I got to the front end of my car and stopped with no further interest in going further because three little 'creatures' came from around behind and stood in front of the object. I think that they were looking at me. I cannot be sure because I did not see eyes of any sort. I know that I was looking at them and I was quite fascinated with what I saw. You might ask why, since I was willing to go up to them before, I did not go up to them now. I used what I hope was common sense. I felt that if they could stop my car, they could surely do something worse to me and I wanted to live to tell the story so that the people of the United States would know that there were things of this nature. I can safely say that we 'looked' at each other for about three minutes. Then they turned and went under the object and a few seconds later, the object started to rise slowly. After it was about one quarter mile high (this is only a guess), the light went out and my car engine started to run again (I did not have to touch the starter), and my headlights came on. I looked at the area that it had been sitting on over and could see no evidence that it had been on the ground. I then drove to the Todd County Sheriff's Office and reported what I had seen to the sheriff. He went back out to the spot and could not find anything on the road that would show they were on the ground. That is what happened. I know that this is quite a wild story but if you do not believe me, well, ———, that's your tough luck."

Many parts of this story were confirmed by others. Several hunters had seen the object and there were four corroborating witnesses to the takeoff.

MISSOURI

CALEDONIA

Both this and the following incident occurred on that fateful date: Wednesday, March 8, 1967. In Caledonia, Mr. J. Sloan Muir saw a flashing light from his kitchen window at 7:15 P.M. He called his wife and they both saw "a shiny, metal, oblong globe, shaped something like a watermelon. Around the perimeter were many beautiful multicolored lights — green and red mostly, but also white, blue, and yellow, running into orange." The Muirs estimated the object to be about thirty-five feet long and said they watched it for fifteen or twenty minutes until it flew out of sight.

BUNCETON

Mrs. Phyllis Rowles of Bunceton said she saw a multicolored object at 8:00 P.M. She described it as having flashing white, green, and blue lights. For two hours it moved in an up-and-down motion. On the same night, Leo Case, a newsman for Station KRMS, was one of the many who reported similar sightings.

OSAGE BEACH and LINN CREEK

The *Versailles Leader-Statesman* of March 16, 1967, reported: "In the past two and one half weeks 75 to 100 persons have reported sightings in the Osage Beach and Linn Creek areas." This time span included the date of March 8.

ST. JOSEPH

Part of a news story that appeared in the St. Joseph *Gazette*, October 9, 1973:

"It was about 10:45, Friday, September 21. It had looked like it might rain earlier in the evening so I stepped to the front window to check the sky.

"Approaching at about treetop level and on a line between the Ackley house and garage on the north was an object of brilliant red and blue light. It passed over the garage and house and then settled toward the lawn, hovering about six feet from the street line about garage-roof high. I heard no sound. For about six minutes it hovered there. I was too petrified to move.

"For a minute or two it was perfectly still. Then very slowly it started to rotate and a sort of ribbed shield came in sight, extending about 10 inches from the side of the circular object up and slanting inward toward the translucent dome."

OHIO

PORTAGE COUNTY

What has been called the "wildest UFO chase on record" took place in Portage County. The object involved was continuously seen by one of several policemen during a seventy-mile chase across two states. The pursuit was sometimes at speeds of up to 105 mph.

The first people to spot the UFO on April 17, 1966, were Deputy Sheriffs Dale F. Spaur and Wilbur Neff. Spaur and Neff saw the UFO come out of a wooded area. Shaped like an ice cream cone and twenty-five to thirty-five feet in diameter, the object was highly illuminated as it moved toward the officers and hovered about one hundred feet above their car. The officers gave chase and were soon joined by another patrol car driven by Officer Wayne Huston about forty miles east near East Palestine, Ohio. Huston had joined in the chase after monitoring the police radio and hearing Spaur's conversation in which he was ordered to follow the "apparition."

The two patrol cars crossed into Pennsylvania in pursuit of the object, which Spaur described as being "as big as a house." At Conway, Pennsylvania, the two cars stopped near the parked Pennsylvania patrol car of Officer Frank Panzanella. The four officers watched the thing suddenly rise rapidly to about 3500 feet. It stopped for a while and then continued up until it disappeared from sight.

Project Blue Book tried to explain the incident by claiming that the officers had first seen a satellite and then somehow transferred their attention to the planet Venus. This was a remarkable theory since, according to Dr. Hynek, first, there was no satellite visible at that time over Ohio, and second, the officers had seen Venus while at the same time seeing the UFO.

ATHENS

On October 18, 1973, the day after Governor Gilligan reported his sighting, three Athens police officers spent about an hour watching the early morning sky as two UFOs hovered over the city. The officers refused to be identified to the local newspaper although they insisted they had all been cold sober. They said that each object was shaped like an "ice cream cone" and hovered in both horizontal and vertical positions from about 12:55 A.M. until they drifted out of sight in a southerly course.

This is an extreme blow-up of a UFO taken by a New Lebanon, Ohio, patrolman in 1973. The object next to the large one is a star. About twenty-five New Lebanon residents watched the object for almost half an hour.

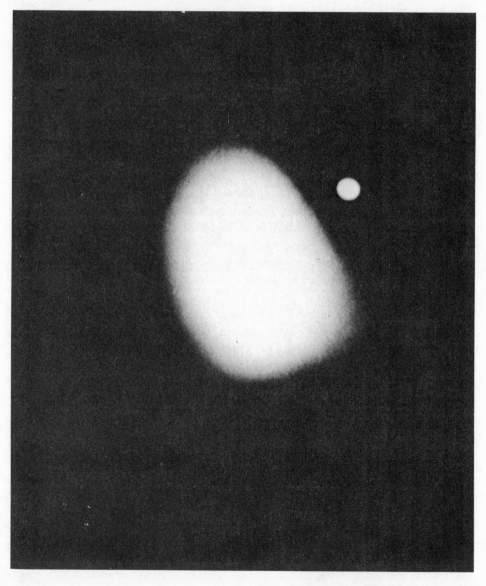

ADAMS COUNTY

On the same morning, Adams County deputies Jerry Blanton and Tony Crawford were on routine patrol when they spotted a UFO hovering about two hundred feet above the ground in the vicinity of Chaperal Road. The deputies watched it for several minutes, awestruck. They had a camera in the car but were too spellbound to think of using it. The object, with brilliant pulsating lights of red, green, blue, and white, moved in a jerky fashion, zigzagging in a very tight circle.

WISCONSIN

MONTICELLO

This is a case where the government investigators were clearly impressed with the obvious mental balance of the witnesses. On April 3, 1964, a young anthropologist and his family were driving about a mile west of Monticello on a small road heading toward Argyle. When they first saw the object, they were neither alarmed nor surprised — two blinking lights low on the horizon would figure to be the red lights of some police cars on a hill. However, as the lights came closer they rose in the sky. The two blinking lights, one red and one green, were followed behind by a large white light. The sighters figured that the object was an airliner about to crash. But the thing didn't crash. Now, still closer, it looked "like a Christmas tree in the night" and covered a large area in the sky. At a distance of one hundred to three hundred yards, it appeared to be an enormous, solid object bearing a considerable number of light sources. It passed by the car and the driver turned around to follow. However, even at the maximum speed limit the car could not keep up. The object rose very high in the sky and became only a diffuse red glow, now way past Monticello. In another minute it was gone.

The Air Force investigation at first considered and then discarded the possibility that a helicopter was involved. The witnesses were concerned and alarmed but in full control of their senses. They could discuss every possibility rationally and dispassionately. Their only report had been to the military and they wanted no publicity. One possible solution after another was quickly abandoned: no helicopter, no police car, no airliner, no mirage, no unusual atmospheric phenomenon, no scientific balloon. Then what was it?

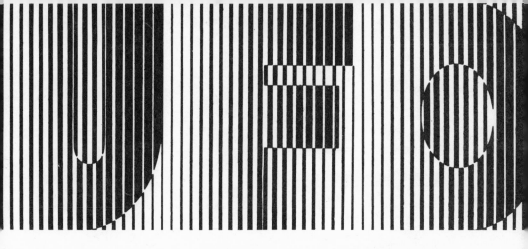

Chapter 7

PLAINS AND MOUNTAIN STATES

Chapter 7
PLAINS AND MOUNTAIN STATES

COLORADO

COLORADO SPRINGS

An incident that even the University of Colorado radar man considered the most baffling radar case on record occurred at the airport at Colorado Springs on May 13, 1967. A UFO was picked up on radar as it neared the airport. Because NORAD Headquarters is in the area, all unidentified objects or aircraft receive immediate attention. Although there were intermittent snow and rain showers, visibility was fair. But the UFO could not be seen, despite some very strong "blips" that clearly indicated a solid craft. The possibility of "ghost echoes" was soon eliminated. The tower operators still had no solution when a Braniff airliner landed. Then radar tracked the invisible UFO to the right. It had come within two hundred feet of the ground over the airport and had still not been seen! Using binoculars, the tower operators could not pick up the UFO.

The University of Colorado radar expert who was called in admitted that he could offer no explanation. There has been speculation that more than any other, this incident has shaken up our Air Force and could account for the lid of secrecy and denial clamped down on UFOs for the last decade. It raised the awesome possibility that the operators of these technically far-advanced UFOs could even make their craft invisible.

IDAHO

RIRIE

Guy Tossie and Willie Begay, two Navajo Indians, were driving on Highway 26 not far from Ririe when a small UFO appeared in the air right be-

fore their car in a blinding flash of light. The vehicle, shaped like two saucers rim to rim, had about an eight-foot diameter and a transparent dome
on top. Tossie and Begay could make out two occupants in the UFO.
Their car was halted and, while green and orange lights flashed, the dome
of the UFO unhinged and a three-and-a-half-foot occupant floated toward
the car. The creature opened the car door and entered. Its face was covered with rough skin and it had high ears, round eyes, no nose, and a mere
slit for a mouth. It was wearing coveralls and some kind of backpack.

Somehow the car was moved into a field and Begay made a run for it,
pursued by one of the aliens. The other strange being tried to converse
with Tossie in unintelligible sounds. Then the occupant who had chased
Begay came back. Both aliens returned to the UFO, which then rose in a
zigzag pattern. While a yellow light flamed, the craft moved off quickly.

About fifteen minutes later, Begay returned with Willard Hammon, a
farmer, and his son. The two startled Indians were taken to the police to
report the bizarre incident. They admitted they had been drinking beer,
but everyone agreed that they were not drunk.

This was not the end of the strange events in Ririe that day. At 11:30
P.M., a truckdriver was stopped by a small UFO which came down in
front of him. A small figure got out of the UFO and tried to enter the
truck, but the driver managed to elude the intruder and drove off.

KANSAS

PITTSBURGH

On August 25, 1952, a lone driver spotted a UFO along a rough gravel
road about a quarter of a mile from U.S. Highway 60 in Pittsburgh. It
was seventy feet long and twelve feet high. There were a number of "windows" and the motorist could see the "man" he believed was controlling
the object. The object eventually flew off, but the important aspect of
this sighting is that there were some physical effects associated with it.
According to Blue Book:

"The object was reported as hovering over an open two-acre field used
for cattle grazing. The general area is heavily wooded. In the field over
which the object hovered, the grass was pressed down forming a circle of
sixty-foot diameter impression with the grass in a recognizable concentric
pattern. Loose grass lay over the top of the impression as if drawn in by
suction when the object ascended vertically at high speed. Vegetation

and grass are approximately four to five feet high. Matted grass was veri-
fied by several witnesses. Samples of soil and grass were sent to Dayton
and analyzed by the Technical Analysis Division with the results that the
samples show no evidence of any radioactivity, burning, or stress of any
kind."

DELPHOS

In a more recent incident — on November 2, 1971 — physical traces more
startling than those of the Pittsburgh encounter were found near Delphos.
An eight-foot ring was apparently left by a rumbling, glowing object, and
soil tests were made at Utah State and Northwestern University and by
private agricultural laboratories. A study of these reports reveals:

"Soil from the ring, compared to the control sample from the ground
nearby: does not absorb water, is more acidic and higher in soluble salts;
contains five to ten times more calcium than the control and somewhat
more minerals (magnesium, potassium); produces less seed growth than
the control, and is coated with a hydrocarbon. . . . The coating of soil
particles is of a material of low atomic weight, with globules of higher
atomic weight imbedded in it. Unique icicle-shaped crystals 0.1 to 0.05
microns long were found, as was a previously uncatalogued crystalline
structure of low atomic weight."

MARION

On March 8, 1967 — there's that date again — several police officers in
Marion observed a UFO between 8:00 and 8:30 P.M. Marion police dis-
patcher Sterling Frame and several others watched it through binoculars
and saw it change colors, from red to green to yellow. As the Marion
County Record of the following day stated: "They all agree they saw it.
There's no question about that."

GOODLAND

Again on March 8, 1967, two top lawmen, Sheriff G. L. Sullivan and Police Chief Al Kisner, observed a twelve- to fourteen-foot-long object with
another object some twelve feet in diameter attached to the bottom of it.
It had three lights, red, amber, and green. On that same evening a Good-
land policeman, Ron Weehunt, reported that he had seen an oval-shaped,
domed object about fifty feet long. It flew over the city at about 1000
to 1500 feet.

MONTANA

STEVENSVILLE

On March 8, 1967 (again!), Mrs. Richard Haagland of Stevensville saw what she described to the Missoula County Sheriff's Office as a circular flying object. She said the object "dropped three balls of fire before disappearing" at 8:20 P.M.

EKALAKA, LAME JONES, and WILLARD

On March 9, 1967, the Fallon County *Times* reported: "Many people have seen unidentified flying objects in the Ekalaka, Lame Jones, and Willard areas. The report is that they seem to hover about a mile from the ground, 'fly' up and down, or in any direction that seems to pleasure them. They are lit up with red and green lights and are apt to be seen in the early night.

"The report to the *Times* office by Mrs. Harry Hanson of Willard relates that Stanley Ketchum has seen them at what seems to be a closer range than most, and any attempt at trying to get close to them makes them literally disappear into thin air."

GREAT FALLS

A rare instance of a UFO being recorded on movie film occurred on August 15, 1950. The film was taken by an amateur photographer, Nicholas Mariana, general manager of the Great Falls Electrics baseball team. It was generally conceded that the photography was not faked, since many reference objects were incorporated. The consensus of opinion was that no aircraft, balloon, or other natural phenomenon could explain the situation. One negative view was stated by anti-UFOer Philip Klass, who said it was caused by two Air Force jets landing at a nearby base. It should be pointed out that the Air Force itself rejected the idea that the sighting was the image of two F-94s. A more important controversy may be that Mariana claimed the first 35 frames of his film submitted to the Air Force were withheld by them. He said these frames clearly showed the objects to be silvery in appearance with a notch at one point on their periphery, and rotating in unison.

NEBRASKA

SIDNEY

July 31, 1965, was an incredible day for sightings in the Midwest and Plains states. Formations of UFOs were witnessed by astronomers, state police, newsmen, and literally thousands of other citizens. Particularly heavy sightings occurred in Oklahoma, Texas, Kansas, and Nebraska. At the ordnance depot in Sidney, Nebraska, a guard captain and other witnesses said they saw a large UFO with four smaller crafts trailing behind it in a diamond formation.

NEVADA

LAS VEGAS

UFO supporters say that Project Blue Book was a sloppy, poorly done investigation. A typical case they cite is a report made of a round, orange object seen on August 12, 1958, about twelve miles northwest of Las Vegas. There was diffuse light in an area where no "treetop level" lights of any kind were ever seen before. The light was reported to have moved down and to the left to treetop level and then back to its original position. The whole routine was then repeated, after which the object vanished.

The Air Force finding in this odd case: "Probably conventional light of some sort."

NORTH DAKOTA

BISMARCK

Two brightly lighted objects caused considerable consternation to three airport tower operators and several other witnesses in Bismarck on November 26, 1968. The tower operators watched as the two bright points performed a series of quick maneuvers and turns. At first one of the lights started heading south while the other traveled north. Suddenly the southbound light executed a 180-degree turn and came back to the other. Then, in formation, the two lights flew off. The tower operators were men of considerable experience, up to twenty-seven years on the job, and they could not attribute the lights to satellites or airplanes or any other so-called natural phenomena.

SOUTH DAKOTA

GLENHAM

In January, 1974, a half-dozen people had an unusual, or perhaps a typical, encounter with a UFO in Glenham. The "usual" appeared to happen. The UFO affected the car's motor and speeded up when the car did. The people in the car turned their vehicle around; the object overhead did likewise. The people made it to their home and went inside for several hours. When they came back outside, they found that the object was still hovering high over the house. Through binoculars, the UFO appeared to have a row of several small windows around it.

The witnesses declined to be identified. This too is a fairly common aspect of UFO encounters. The general theory is that UFO hoaxers make up their stories for the public attention they get. Then what can be the possible motives of people who refuse to be identified? Of course, one may say that they obtain sufficient gratification just from the turmoil they create; however, it seems more likely that they had a genuine experience and felt a duty to report it, but did what they could to prevent public ridicule if they were identified.

UTAH

TREMONTON

On July 2, 1952, Officer Delbert C. Newhouse, a Navy chief photographer, and his wife and two children had just driven through the small town of Tremonton, north of Salt Lake City. Newhouse's wife first spotted a group of about a dozen unusual objects maneuvering in the sky. Newhouse, a man with one thousand hours of aerial photographic missions to his credit, reacted instinctively. Pulling over to the side of U.S. Highway 30S, he grabbed a 16mm Bell & Howell movie camera and began shooting film of the strange objects at about 10,000 feet.

No film was ever more intensely gone over than the Newhouse film, because it had been taken by a man of such impeccable character. It was subjected to over one thousand man-hours of analysis in the U.S. Navy photographic laboratory at Anacostia, Maryland, and intensive study at the Air Force photo lab at Wright-Patterson Air Force Base. Eventually, the Air Force classified the UFOs as "possible birds." This was done despite the finding by the Air Force lab that the brightness of the images on the film exceeded that of any bird. The Navy concurred that no bird was known to reflect enough light to cause the images produced on the Newhouse film. There was a proposal that the Air Force and Navy redo the film by shooting movies of sea gulls in an attempt to match the brightness of the Newhouse film. The Air Force opted instead for a "finding" that the objects were "possible birds."

WYOMING

CHEYENNE

On August 1, 1965, Cheyenne, Wyoming, was the site of a rash of UFO reports. A large, multicolored disc was sighted by a number of Air Force personnel. Then five glowing objects and two other objects were sighted by other Air Force witnesses. This was followed by yet another sighting of a large white ovoid with a flashing red light. This sighting was to the west of Cheyenne and the witnesses were, again, Air Force people. All in all, it was a rather embarrassing day for the Air Force, which later claimed there were no such things as UFOs.

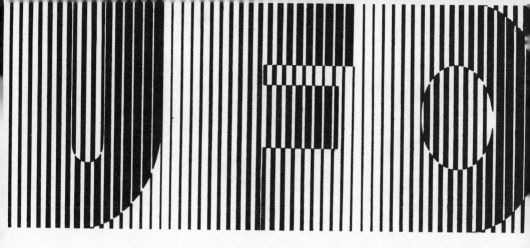

Chapter 8
THE WEST COAST

This California UFO was photographed from the window of a truck.

Chapter 8

THE WEST COAST

CALIFORNIA

CISCO GROVE

On September 5, 1964, 27-year-old Don Shrum, out on a bow-and-arrow hunting trip, became separated from his two companions. As night fell, Shrum decided to take shelter in a tree. He strapped himself to a twelve-foot branch to prevent his falling while asleep. It was then that Shrum saw three flying objects with protruding and rotating lights. At first he assumed they were helicopters searching for him, so he climbed down from the tree and lit a fire. Shrum saw a flash and a dark object landing, apparently about 450 yards away.

He climbed back up the tree and tried to locate the object. He then saw a "dome-shaped affair" that was no helicopter, and two creatures about five and one-half feet tall, dressed in a silvery-grey material. Shrum could make out no facial features.

The pair approached Shrum's signal fires. He could now make out large, protruding eyes and heard them apparently communicating with some sort of cooing sound. They were soon joined by a third creature, who moved much more clumsily and seemed robotlike. According to Shrum, the three spotted him in the tree and tried to dislodge him. Desperately, he fired some arrows and hit the "robot." This produced some sparks but did not deter the aliens from still trying to dislodge him. Shrum threw his canteen at them and they picked it up and examined it. Then he threw down his bow and some coins. In desperation he set his cap, oversuit, and jacket on fire and threw them at his "attackers." This made them back off for a time.

Toward dawn, a second "robot" appeared on the scene. The two robots then gave off sparks and there was a glow between them. A cloud of gas rose and engulfed Shrum and he passed out. When he awoke, the four aliens were gone. Nauseated and worn out, he climbed down from the tree and wandered about until one of his companions found him. He was informed that one of them had seen the craft the night before.

97

OREGON

McMINNVILLE

On May 11, 1950, in McMinnville, a farmer named Paul Trent took a photograph of a UFO. It has been described as "among the earliest and least 'deauthenticated' in Ufology."

The photo-analyst who evaluated the Trent-McMinnville UFO photos for the Condon Committee reported: "This is one of the few UFO reports in which all factors investigated, geometric, psychological, and physical, appear to be consistent with the assertion that an extraordinary flying object, silvery, metallic, disc-shaped, tens of meters in diameter, and evidently artificial, flew within sight of the two witnesses."

This report was confirmed in a later reexamination by Dr. Bruce Maccabee. The Maccabee finding, based on a detailed photogrammetric study, was that the McMinnville UFO could not have been a small object shot near the camera; it was shot at a considerable distance and hence not a fake.

If it was not a fake, what *was* it?

Two of the Paul Trent photographs taken near McMinnville, Oregon. Subjected to detailed photometric studies and labeled not hoaxes, they are now recognized as being about the least "disproved" of all UFO photos.

WASHINGTON

LYNDEN

Shortly after midnight on January 12, 1965, Department of Justice Inspector Robert E. Kerringer was on patrol duty in Lynden. He was driving at about 40 mph when a bright glow lit up the ground. "It was so powerful," Kerringer later reported to Maj. Donald E. Keyhoe (USMC Ret.), a leading investigator of UFOs, "I could see farm buildings in the distance. I was about to stop and get out when this huge shining thing swooped down, right over the car. It scared me half to death — I was almost paralyzed. The thing was round, about thirty feet in diameter, but the glare was so blinding I couldn't see any details. When it stopped, just above the road, it was less than fifty feet from me. I'd already hit the brakes, but I thought sure I'd ram it."

Kerringer fully expected a crash, but the UFO veered upward out of the way. "I jumped out and saw it hovering above me. I was so rattled that I pulled my revolver, but something kept me from firing."

The strange object remained over Kerringer's car for some three minutes. Kerringer reported that the machine hung there motionless. He felt he was being watched. He saw no pilot and could not tell if the craft was being operated from within or by remote control. Then, suddenly, faster than any jet he had ever seen, the disc shot upward and vanished in the clouds.

Two other Department of Justice officers had also sighted the disc, and it had been tracked by radar at Blaine Air Force Base.

An officer at Blaine warned Kerringer to keep quite about the incident, but since the Air Force has no authority over the Department of Justice, Kerringer decided to go public.

He said, "The Air Force is making a big mistake trying to hide this. It could blow up right in their faces. People should be warned that such things can happen. I didn't believe UFOs were real. I had to be shown, and believe me, it was a rough way to learn."

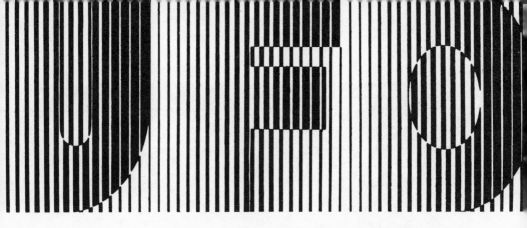

Chapter 9

THE NORTHEAST

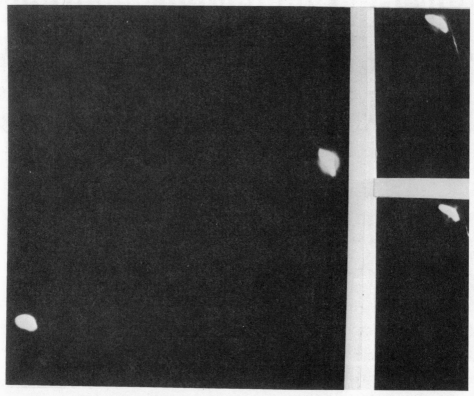

A 1965 photograph of a UFO sighted in Norwich, Connecticut. In the large picture the object is to the right, the moon to the left. The two small pictures are other views of the strange object.

Chapter 9

THE NORTHEAST

CONNECTICUT

SHELTON

This seems to have been the "last leg" of a single set of UFOs sighted in four different spots on August 19, 1959. At about 3:37 P.M., a radar station recorded seven unidentified echoes eighty miles off the Atlantic coast around Washington, D.C. At 6:55 P.M., a woman spotted a vertical luminous red object about six miles west of Mitchell Air Force Base on Long Island, New York. Then, at 7:45 P.M., a man in Trenton, New Jersey, saw an object of unusual brightness just above the horizon to the southeast. He described the object as an elongated vertical cigar, orange in the center and surrounded by a bluish-green area. He then realized that the main object had at least five other shining objects surrounding it. They headed off to the northeast. Finally, at 9:10 P.M., the object appeared over Shelton. It seemed to resemble a first-magnitude star, and it was followed by a spiral trajectory.

DELAWARE

DOVER

It seemed as though just about everybody in Dover saw the UFO on Sunday evening, October 14, 1973. Three women on their way to the market spent forty-five minutes watching a brilliant object cavorting in the sky.

Flight controllers at Dover Air Force Base saw it, too. And an unidentified flying object showed up on radar at the base. The police were called and they also saw it. A Delaware State Police helicopter was sent up to give chase, and the crew was able to zero in on the UFO and follow it for fourteen miles across Kent County. The UFO easily outdistanced the chopper and, changing colors from yellowish-orange to red, disappeared in the night.

MAINE

BANGOR

On March 23, 1966, a motorist named John T. King was driving near Bangor when, he recounted later to police, he observed a domed flying disc on the ground just off the highway. The strange disc was moving towards him and as it came closer his car lights dimmed and his radio went off. Considering himself in mortal danger, the motorist aimed his Magnum pistol at the approaching object. When it was within fifty feet of his car, he opened fire, getting off three shots before the strange disc soared off "at tremendous speed."

MASSACHUSETTS

SUDBURY

A housewife in Sudbury collected samples of a strange material which landed in a 1500-foot circumference on October 22, 1973, while a glowing silvery globe passed overhead. Three other persons saw the strange sticky substance descend. A number of laboratories conducted tests on the material and one reported that the substance had the same amino acid as is found in spider webs. However, experts couldn't agree on the likelihood of such an amount of spider webs suddenly showing up in one spot. There was also disagreement over the possibility that the silvery ball in the sky could have been a congealed mass of spider web.

PROVINCETOWN

A very unusual radar sighting was made on September 21, 1950, by a Massachusetts Institute of Technology radar observer who later reported as follows:

"An exceedingly puzzling event occurred during the 3rd run when the planes were heading northeast at 30,000 feet. We picked up another plane (?) in the radar beam traveling about due north on a converging course toward the F-86s. It was moving very rapidly and I told the pilots about it, its range and direction from them. The echo caught up with, passed, and then crossed the course of the 86s, suddenly went into a very tight (for the speed) turn to the *right*, headed back toward Boston and passed *directly over our flight*. (Perhaps went under.) The sketch represents, as closely as we can remember, the relative positions of the two planes. Two other observers were with me at the time and we have checked over the facts rather closely. The pilots will undoubtedly recall the incident. They said they didn't see anything, which is not too surprising considering the speed of the object and the fact that it may have passed several thousand feet above or below them and still looked like coincidence to the radar. Figuring *conservatively*, the speed of the object was approximately 1200 mph, and the centrifugal force exerted on the ship during the turn amounted to something more than five *g*'s. . . . The turn was utterly fantastic, I don't think the human frame could absorb it, but if the object was radio controlled, it had no particular business flying on such courses as planes occupied on legitimate business. A few rough calculations concerning control surfaces, angles, etc., only add to the puzzle that this object must have been entirely unconventional in many and basic respects. . . . It seems highly probable that I may be poking into something that is none of my business, but on the other hand, it may be something that the Air Force would like to know about if it doesn't already. I wish you would take the matter up with your intelligence officer or C.O. and get their reactions. The whole thing has us going nuts here and we don't know whether to talk about it or keep our mouths shut. Until I hear from you we will do the latter. . . . "

The radar man was advised that the Air Force would get in touch with him, but it never did. Was it because the Air Force knew too much . . . or too little?

NEW HAMPSHIRE

ENFIELD - WILMOT

At 10:00 P.M. on January 15, 1965, Charles Knee, Jr., of Concord suddenly found his car engine stalling on the road between Enfield and Wilmot. The car lights went off. Knee got out of the car and heard a high-pitched sound and saw a bright light cross the sky. But the encounter got no closer.

THE WHITE MOUNTAINS

Perhaps the most famous close encounter with a UFO — certainly the most written about — was the experience of Betty and Barney Hill, an interracial couple from New Hampshire. On September 19, 1961, the Hills were motoring along Route 3, returning home to Portsmouth after a vacation in Canada. Betty was the first to notice a bright object in the night sky. At first the couple figured the light was merely a very bright star. As the object grew larger they decided it was a man-made satellite. It got even closer and they were sure now it was a plane. But the bright object hovered above them little more than a city block from their car. It could not be a plane.

Barney Hill got out of the car and focused his binoculars on the hovering machine (that much it definitely was). Hill could clearly distinguish at least six living beings behind a bank of windows. Fear crept through Hill's body. He turned and ran toward the car. He screamed to Betty as he jumped into the front seat and threw the vehicle into gear. Barney gunned the car along the deserted road until the couple heard an electronic type of beeping from behind them. Suddenly everything went hazy. They were to remember very little of what had transpired until much later, when they were within seventeen miles of Concord on Route 93. For two hours there was a total blank. Their memories returned only after they found themselves thirty-five miles from where they last remembered being.

The experience haunted the couple and they sought psychiatric treatment. Under hypnosis they told a strange story, recorded in meticulous detail in an article in *Look* magazine by John Fuller, who then went into it in greater depth in a now famous book, *The Interrupted Journey*. The

Mr. and Mrs. Barney Hill holding a copy of the book telling about their ordeal of being captured and examined by eerie occupants of a UFO.

Hills, under hypnosis, told of being taken aboard the alien craft and given thorough physical examinations by small creatures with wide, slanted eyes, pointed chins, and mere slits for mouths. An instrument was placed over Barney's genitals. (Later, a ring of warts erupted around his groin.) Betty Hill described how the creatures inserted a long needle into her navel. When she expressed her fear that it would be painful, she was told it would not hurt and was simply a test for pregnancy.

The creatures communicated by making odd sounds, but somehow these were translated into English in the couple's thoughts. The couple was informed that they would forget the experience and were then returned to their car.

NEW JERSEY

HACKENSACK

At least a dozen residents of Hackensack, including a policeman, said they saw a UFO hover over the city for a half hour in early October, 1973. According to one witness: "There was a reddish beam of light coming down. There were three lights, red, green, and white, and when I looked through the binoculars it was spinning."

WOODCLIFF LAKE

On June 4, 1974, Robert J. LeDonne, editor of the Special Events Unit of ABC News, spotted a "brilliant oval of lights" at 9:05 P.M. A rear red light and a number of bright yellow lights revolved around the object. LeDonne heard no sound, even when the craft was at treetop level, which eliminated the possibility of its being a helicopter. He watched the craft "dip abruptly, then return to its normal altitude." After a few minutes LeDonne watched the UFO vanish behind a treetop. He notified the police and was told that a local police car had previously reported a UFO in the same vicinity.

PARSIPPANY and CALDWELL

Whatever it was, it was not Fourth of July fireworks. At 12:05 A.M. on July 4, 1975, a college student and his girlfriend were returning home from the movies in Parsippany when they saw a light, different from any other they had ever seen. It illuminated the surrounding area, yet somehow had no glare. As the object moved closer they saw that specific colors were being emitted from different parts of the craft — red, white, and blue-green. After the strange machine maneuvered and hovered above for several minutes, it suddenly "whizzed off" in the space of a second.

At 10:00 P.M. that same evening another couple approached private pilot Jim Quodomine at Caldwell Field. The couple pointed out a UFO to Quodomine and his fiancee. Because he had never seen a light of this type before, Quodomine decided to give chase. He and his fiancee took off in one of the planes and at a height of 3000 feet came within four or five miles of the object. Quodomine tried to move closer at a speed of 100 mph, but the object changed brightness and, picking up speed, disappeared in a matter of seconds.

NEW YORK

CHERRY CREEK

Despite the rather outlandish statements made in the Cherry Creek report, even Blue Book did not label it a hoax. According to the Blue Book summary, on August 19, 1965:

"The witness was working in a barn (a few minutes after sunset) when he noticed unusual AM radio interference plus a beeping sound. When he went outside he saw an object which he described as being saucer-shaped like two plates lip to lip. The object was described as fifty feet long and twenty feet thick and its color was shiny silver with red glowing streamers projecting downward from the entire perimeter plus a trail from red to yellow color. The object appeared to land near the farm and when the observer sighted it, the object rapidly ascended into the clouds. The clouds then turned green (color of tree leaves) and an odor like burning gasoline from the object was also noted.

"Forty-five minutes later the object reappeared (this time observed by a second witness) descending slowly from the clouds towards a wooded area and then almost immediately rose again into the clouds leaving a dim red trail. The clouds again turned green near the object. The object reappeared at nine p.m. (half an hour later) descending towards the surface. It then rose to a height below the clouds and moved away SSW all the while emitting a yellow trail. The object was reported to have caused reduction in the milk from the farmer's cow from two and a half cans to one can, disturbed a bull in a field, and caused a dog to bark."

When the original sighting was made it was investigated by the State Police from the Chautauqua County Police Barracks and then by an investigating officer and technicians from the Niagara Falls Municipal Airport. The police report reads in part:

"The saucer-shaped object is reported to look like two dinner plates held face to face, silvery and very shiny, fifty feet long and twenty feet thick. It was reported that a bull tethered near the barn became so frightened that it bent the iron bar in the ground to which it was tethered. After the parents of the boy were questioned as well as the neighbors, regarding the character and reliability of the boys, the investigating officer and three technicians were convinced that the sighting was not a hoax or fabrication. The fourth technician remained unconvinced."

The boys were subsequently subjected to "polite but vigorous questioning," but never wavered from their story. A beeping radio, a barking dog, a frightened bull, a poorly producing milk cow . . . not exactly what Project Blue Book liked to believe in. But even the Air Force could not find anything to support a hoax theory, and the case was labeled "Unidentified."

NEW YORK CITY

On June 4, 1978, scores of people in Brooklyn and Queens saw what they said was a UFO. An official of the Federal Aviation Agency at Kennedy Airport saw the eerie lights hanging in the southwest sky for about three minutes until they vanished. "It was not a normal star sighting," he said.

A Brooklyn mail clerk, Steve Horvatt, sky-gazing from his Ralph Avenue stoop, watched unmoving mysterious lights for almost two hours. When he climbed to his roof for a better view, they had disappeared. "I've never seen stars like that before. And they didn't move like a plane or satellite."

Dan Noonan was taking pictures on the roof of the fourteen-story New York University Medical School dorm along the East River at 3:00 P.M. He said, "I was looking down at the FDR Drive when I saw something flying around that at first I thought was a frisbee. It couldn't have been bigger than three feet across. It was round and white. But it wasn't acting like a bird or something floating in the wind. It was flying — but it made absolutely no noise." The 26-year-old medical student watched for five minutes while the UFO was in sight. It rose to the level of the roof, "hovered" over the middle of the East River, then "took off" in the direction of Kennedy Airport, reflecting the sun metallically as it went. Noonan added: "I thought it was a UFO at the time. But I wasn't willing to admit it to myself until I'd heard other people had seen something."

The night-viewed UFO was given one explanation by pilot Bernard Faraino, who thought people had seen *him* buzzing the Brooklyn shoreline with his night-light advertisement for "Randazzo's Seafood Restaurant, Sheepshead Bay." He explained, "You can only see that there are letters and words when you're directly below the plane. From anywhere else, all you see is a stream of bright, flashing lights. That's when I'm over the shore. But when I circle back over the water, I cut all the lights on the billboard and plane — that explains the disappearance. I can't blame the people for going out of their minds. It does look like a flying saucer, especially as I climb. But that's why this unit is made this way. It's supposed to attract attention."

Naturally, such an explanation would be seized upon by UFO debunkers for an entry in a book "explaining" UFOs, but it does not really explain much. Both the FAA officer and the mail clerk, Steve Horvatt, were not at all convinced that they saw a Cessna 150 with a forty-foot grid of 375 bulbs. The time frame matches, but not the description. "I would have seen the motion if that was it," the FAA officer said. "No, these lights were stationary, about 30 degrees off the horizon, west-southwest. They gave all the appearances of being stars — but they vanished."

And of course the Faraino solution has nothing to do with the daytime "sky phantoms" seen by Noonan and others.

PENNSYLVANIA

PALMERTON

On May 26, 1964, a "stationary object with a dome whose interior edges emitted a whitish light" was seen by members of two Palmerton families. There was a smaller object shaped like a disc, maneuvering around the large one. Then the smaller one seemed to merge into the main craft, which then disappeared to the east.

ECONOMY

At 9:40 P.M. on May 27, 1965, a resident of Economy watched for two minutes as a strange object cavorted in the sky. It seemed to be made up of two large spheres, one at each end, with perhaps three or four smaller spheres between. The strange object was definitely spinning or rotating from left to right. It seemed to be tipped at an angle of about 15 degrees, which permitted a three-dimensional view.

With such a definite sighting, Project Blue Book's conclusion seems almost sobbingly given: "Aircraft. Sighting characteristic of aircraft. No attempt at specific identification. Regarded as possible aircraft sighting. No data presented to indicate object could NOT have been an aircraft."

RHODE ISLAND

Poor little Rhode Island! No UFOs. In a recent study made of "revised unidentifieds" — elimination of sightings for which an explanation has been found — it turned out that Rhode Island was the site of 0.0 percent of the UFO sightings. Rhode Island is a blank but, happily for the UFO hunter, it is a tiny state and easily traversed.

VERMONT

BETHEL

During the great UFO flap of 1965, Dr. R. S. Woodruff, the state pathologist, and a high state police official were riding in a police car near Bethel when a UFO started red-lighting them from overhead. Behind this UFO two others followed, holding to the same altitude and course and at precise intervals. The sighting was witnessed as well by drivers of cars behind the police vehicle. The officials placed the speed of the three UFOs at about 2000 mph.

The Pentagon tried to debunk the sightings by declaring that the objects were "meteors." The reaction to this explanation was about as bad as the one to the Michigan "swamp gas" theory. Meteors fall at a rate far greater than 2000 mph, and they come down in helter-skelter fashion. It is not possible that they would descend together, slow down, and then level off in practically parade formation. The Pentagon's explanation led the highly respected television commentator Frank Edwards to remark: "You'd do a lot better, gentlemen, if you'd draw your answers out of a hat."

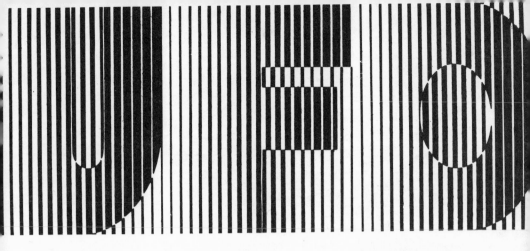

Chapter 10
WRAPPING UP

Chapter 10
WRAPPING UP

ALASKA

DOUGLAS ISLAND

Our most northerly state has seen its share of UFOs and has one locale categorized by the local press as "historically a favorite resting place for unidentified flying objects." A typical sighting at the location, Douglas Island, occurred on August 14, 1973, when at least half a dozen inhabitants of the tiny, offshore island spotted a motionless "small glowing object" overhead before it disappeared at about 11:00 P.M. Two of the witnesses were able to study the twenty-minute UFO visit through a telescope, which made the sighting all the more accurate. One of them, Wayne Smallwood, Jr., related: "I looked . . . and it looked like a bright boiled egg yolk with a needle stuck through it. The points on each side were giving off a glow which would get brighter, then duller."

HAWAII

OFFSHORE

In April, 1952, Secretary of the Navy Dan Kimball was flying to Hawaii when two strange disc-shaped craft suddenly rushed at his plane. "Their speed was amazing," Kimball told Maj. Donald Keyhoe. "My pilots estimated it between fifteen hundred and two thousand miles an hour. The objects circled us twice and then took off, heading east. There was another Navy plane behind us, with Admiral Arthur Radford on board. The distance was about fifty miles. I had my senior pilot radio a report on the sighting. In almost no time Radford's chief pilot called back, really excited. The UFOs were now circling their plane — they'd covered the fifty miles in less than two minutes. In a few seconds the pilot told us they'd left the plane and raced up out of sight."

Secretary Kimball ordered that a report be made to the Air Force, since it was in charge of investigating UFOs. Later, there seems little doubt that Kimball was convinced that the Air Force was involved in a cover-up operation. He ordered the Navy to conduct its own investigations of UFO sightings involving Navy and Marine personnel. (See the Newhouse-Utah sighting.)

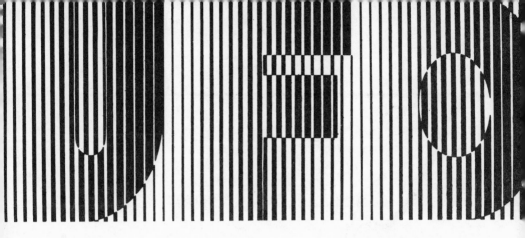

Chapter 11

UFOs NORTH OF THE BORDER

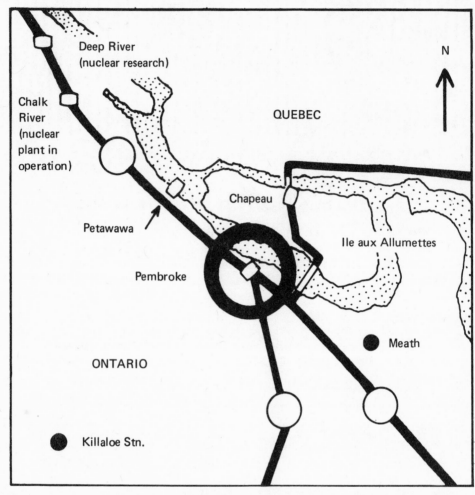

This map shows Canada's No. 1 UFO hot spot, the town of Pembroke, which is circled.

Chapter 11

UFOs NORTH OF THE BORDER

Canada is a vacationland for United States tourists and for UFOs as well. Reports of Canadian UFO sightings would fill a book of their own. We will cover just a few areas, including a town that can rightly be called the "UFO Hot Spot of Canada."

FALCON LAKE, MANITOBA

A lone witness to a UFO landing at Falcon Lake, Manitoba, on May 20, 1967, was treated for first-degree abdominal burns. He said he had been knocked down by a hot blast of air when he tried to look through the opening of a landed UFO.

PEMBROKE

Through the years an astonishing number of UFO encounters have taken place along the Ontario side of the Ottawa River, particularly around Pembroke, a town of about 17,000 residents lying directly opposite Allumettes Island and a few miles south of the Deep River nuclear research laboratory and the Chalk River nuclear power plant.

At 3:30 A.M., Sunday, July 13, 1969, Edgar Paquette was driving along a small road outside Pembroke with a female friend. Suddenly, the road "lit up like day." When the couple looked back, they saw a bright light that seemed to be following them.

"I always thought I had guts," Paquette said later, "but I was never so scared in my life. It seemed to be aimed right at us."

He stopped the car and got out, finding his curiosity getting the better of his fear. He began signalling the object with a flashlight as it passed by very low. Paquette noted that the object was about eight feet in diameter and seemed to have two legs suspended from it. When the object dropped to about sixty feet from the ground, panic returned to Paquette. He jumped back into his car and headed for the nearest house, that of Mr. and Mrs. Gerry Chartrand. Paquette's companion cried out to the Chartrands, "Have you got a phone? My God, have you got a phone?"

Two constables and three military policemen responded to the call for assistance, and they too witnessed the strange sky visitor. Constable Jack McKay said, "It was really bright. There wasn't another thing in the sky and it was dawn before it disappeared."

McKay and Constable Grant Chaplin chased the object for thirty-eight minutes as it headed southeast. Meanwhile, back in Pembroke, John Chasson, a taxi driver, saw the object. He reported that it was much brighter than a star and appeared to be oval-shaped.

Edward Paquette had not waited around for the police pursuit. He returned to his home and the strange object appeared to have followed him. It hovered over the Paquette home and was seen by his son and daughter, Sam and Gloria Ann. "The four of us drove as far as the gate and then the light came down at us again," Paquette said. "It didn't bother us after that, but Gloria Ann had run back into the house, she was scared."

This was hardly an isolated incident around Pembroke. In May, 1969, a farmer named Leo Paul Chaput was sitting in the kitchen with his wife and two of their ten children. It was 2:00 A.M. when they saw a sudden flash in a field some 130 yards from the house. When they stepped outside to investigate, they had to throw their hands over their faces to protect their eyes from the intense glare. The glare was coming from four luminous objects they judged to be at least thirty feet in diameter and sixteen feet high. The objects hovered just a few feet from the ground for about five or six minutes before vanishing. As they moved off, farmer Chaput was aware of a noise, something akin to the chugging of a boat motor.

At daylight, Chaput went out to inspect the field where he had seen the eerie flash. The grass was still burning in a few spots. He found four circular patterns twenty-seven feet in diameter, each about two feet wide. Inside one of the circles two small trees were singed and smoldering. Over the next several weeks, the strange objects returned to the Chaput farm on a number of occasions. They gave off a bright orange light as they passed about 500 feet overhead each time.

Then, almost a month later, on June 2, 1969, a scorched circle was found on John McLaren's farm outside Meath, Ontario, not far from the Ottawa River and Allumettes Island. This circle was about thirty feet in diameter and also had a two-foot-wide ring. Mrs. McLaren reported, "The circle wasn't there on Sunday, June 1st, because we would have noticed it. It must have happened after everyone was asleep and that was past 1 a.m."

ASBESTOS - DRUMMONDVILLE

The Montreal, Quebec, sector has also had numerous UFO encounters. In August, 1968, alone, more than sixty sightings were reported by some

This photograph of a UFO was taken by three witnesses in the Canadian Rockies. Investigators found no evidence of a hoax.

250 witnesses in areas such as Thetford Mines, Black Lake, Coleraine, Disraeli, Vimy Ridge, St. Ferdinande de' Halifax, Ste-Julie, St-Adrien, and St-Robert. In Vimy Ridge, the UFOs came slowly up the side of a mountain, twisting around the trees and valleys, apparently under very intelligent control.

The most amazing stories concern sightings in Drummondville and Asbestos. In Drummondville, eight witnesses came forward to say they had seen a UFO occupant walking stiffly in robotlike fashion. And in Asbestos, according to the *Sherbrook La Tribune* of October 9, 1968, a family was watching television when the wife suddenly screamed to her husband, "Paul, hurry, look!" The husband rushed outside the house and saw a strange rectangular green object in the sky. It seemed to be illuminated from behind. After a few minutes, the object grew much brighter and greener. Then a saucer-shaped object encircled by a yellow-orange light came out of a cloud.

The husband and his brother-in-law got into their car and drove off in the direction of the objects. The saucer then seemed to incline to the right and change its position, vanishing behind a cloud which then turned green. As the men kept driving, a "truly dazzling ball of yellow-orange came out of a cloud." They came across some boys walking in a field and all of them had to shield their eyes because the light had turned so blindingly bright that they could not see through the glare.

Back at the house, the wife and her sister could still see the objects. Both swore they saw what appeared to be two humanlike figures glide out of the saucer and seemingly walk in mid-air. At last, the lights slowly veered off in the direction of Windsor, Quebec, and disappeared.

Clearly, from anywhere in America, a UFO hunter can go east, west, north, or south and discover the bizarre and unexplained in unidentified flying saucers. Happy hunting!

EPILOGUE

"Interest in UFOs has now reversed and is increasing at all levels in the military. There have just been too many UFO sightings and too many fighters scramble to chase them. I have been around a fraternity of pilots for a long time. I have talked with pilots who have been involved in scrambling after UFOs. Fighters have spotted things but couldn't catch them." — *Apollo astronaut Edgar Mitchell*

"If I become President, I'll make every piece of information this country has about UFO sightings available to the public and the scientists." — *Jimmy Carter*

"The President is just ignoring legitimate demands by the American public that they be informed of this area of vital importance." — *U.S. Rep. Mario Biaggi (D.-N.Y.)*

MAJOR AMERICAN UFO ORGANIZATIONS

Aerial Phenomena Research Organization (APRO)
3910 East Kleindale Road
Tuscon, Arizona 85712

Founded by Jim and Coral Lorenzen in 1952, APRO is the oldest UFO organization in the United States. Jim Lorenzen is international director, Coral Lorenzen is secretary-treasurer, and Dr. James A. Harder is research director.

This group conducts field investigations, sponsors conferences, and prints an abundance of UFO news in its monthly *APRO Bulletin*. In addition, the Lorenzens have published a number of books on UFOs.

Center for UFO Studies (CUFOS)
P.O. Box 11
Northfield, Illinois 60093

CUFOS was founded in January, 1974, by Dr. J. Allen Hynek, who is its director. Utilizing a string of researchers around the country, CUFOS can have an observer on the scene very quickly. Law enforcement officials have access to a toll-free UFO hot line to report sightings. CUFOS also maintains close working contacts with the Aerial Phenomena Research Organization.

Hynek is probably the most scientific member of the "establishment" ever to swing over to a belief in UFOs. Chairman of the Department of Astronomy at Northwestern University and director of the Lindeheimer Astronomical Research Center located there, Hynek, for twenty-two years, until 1969, was chief scientific consultant on Unidentified Flying Objects to the USAF. His transformation from UFO skeptic was slow, but by the late 1960s he had been "converted." His primary criticism of Blue Book and the Condon Committee was their method of delving into UFO mysteries. He says, "Today I would not spend one further moment on the subject of UFOs if I didn't seriously feel that the UFO phenomenon is real and that efforts to investigate and understand it, and eventually to solve it, could have a profound effect — perhaps even be the springboard to a revolution in mankind's outlook on the universe."

Mutual UFO Network (MUFON)
103 Oldtowne Road
Seguin, Texas 78155

The international director of MUFON is Walter H. Andrus, Jr., and the deputy director is John F. Schuessler.

MUFON stages an annual symposium and publishes a monthly bulletin called *Skylook*. The group has one thousand investigators around the world, mostly in the United States and Canada. All sighting reports are passed on to the Center for UFO Studies for analysis and compilation.

National Investigations Committee on Aerial Phenomena (NICAP)
3535 University Boulevard West
Kensington, Maryland 20795

NICAP was founded in 1956 and has fought a long and public battle with the Air Force, demanding a freer and more extensive study of UFOs. Its board chairman and president is John L. Acuff and its board of governors includes a large number of prominent political and retired military men. NICAP cooperates with the Center for UFO Studies and publishes a monthly bulletin, *UFO Investigator*. Its most prominent director was Donald E. Keyhoe, a former Marine Corps major and aviation writer.

* * * *

A report made to any of these groups will most likely receive an unbiased and thorough examination. It may well be that the mystery of UFOs will be solved not by the United States government but by the research and dedication of such organizations.

INDEX